*Enjoy
Suree Coates*

COOK THAI

WITH
Suree Coates

First published in Great Britain in 2013 by
www.awaywithmedia.com, Shrewsbury SY3 7LN
© Suree Coates

ISBN
978-0-9576292-1-9

All rights reserved. No part of this publication may be reproduced or utilised in any form by any means, electronic or mechanical, including photocopying, recording or by any information storage and retrieval system, without prior permission of the publisher.

Written, photographed and published by
Andrew Richardson

Editorial production
Adam Haynes

foreword

Suree Coates with Will Holland.

Mesmerised. That single word describes the way I felt when I first met Suree Coates.

We were both on the line-up of chefs demonstrating at the Ludlow Food Festival. I arrived early for my demonstration and a big crowd was already gathered around the main stage. Who was causing all the commotion?

Suree had taken centre stage and she was busily working with a watermelon. Within what seemed like minutes, she transformed the large fruit into the most beautiful sculpture. I'd never seen anything like it. I stood, transfixed. She took my breath away. She started with a watermelon and effortlessly turned it into a dragon!

I admired the way she worked from the start: the moment I saw her carve that watermelon. It was her skill level that impressed me the most. As a chef, I instantly recognised her dedication and commitment. And she made me smile. There she was, up on the stage, a crazy little Thai lady entertaining the crowds with a lively display of her craft.

Suree and I are both based in Shropshire. I heard about her not long after arriving in the county, and more recently she proved her worth when she was named the UK's best in a national competition.

I'm a massive fan of Thai food. It's a cuisine that I love to eat when I'm not at work. There are so many things to enjoy about it: it's light, fresh, fragrant, punchy and aromatic. You can eat lots and not get full, which is a bonus, and of course it's very healthy.

My own style of cuisine is based on many different influences and I am frequently inspired by Thai gastronomy. I love the balance of flavours, with sweet and sour, salty and spicy, sharp and hot. Thai food is all about harnessing those brilliant combinations – and chefs like Suree do it brilliantly.

As I've got to know Suree, I've gained enormous respect for her. She runs her restaurant with her family – her husband Simon and son Ross are ever-present in her life. They have supported her dream of being recognised as one of the best Thai chefs in the business.

It's a great privilege to be asked to write the foreword for Suree's debut cookery book. I hope you take inspiration from her work, as I have. And most importantly, I hope you enjoy recreating her dishes in your own home.

WILL HOLLAND
Ludlow, 2013

ABOUT THE AUTHOR
Will Holland was chef patron at the multi-award-winning La Bécasse restaurant, in Ludlow, from 2007 to 2013. He won three rosettes from the AA Restaurant Guide *and a Michelin star within 18 months of its launch. His Acorn Award from the industry recognised his exceptional talent and he consistently features in the UK's top 50 restaurants.* The Good Food Guide *named him one of the ten most influential chefs of the present decade.*

contents

about Suree	8
ingredients	10
sauces/pastes	15
soups	26
starters	32
fish	54
meat	74
rice, noodles, vegetables	96
desserts	116
petits fours	138
decoration	152

Food is in my blood. It's all I've ever done, all I've ever known. In some ways, it's a kind of religion. It's what I do when I want to relax; it's what I do when I go to work; it's what I give my family, to show them how much I love them.

Most chefs disappear from the kitchen when it's their day off. And why wouldn't they? We chefs work extraordinarily long hours in hot, difficult conditions. It's no wonder chefs like to let off steam.

I don't, however. On days when the restaurant is closed, on high days and holidays, you'll find me in the kitchen. That's the time when I'm able to experiment with new dishes and new flavours. It's the time when I'm able to perfect my desserts, or find out about new flavours and combinations. It's the time when I'm able to create the next special dish that my customers will love.

I often feel as though I'm the luckiest person in the world. I love cooking and I get to do it every day. And my family – Simon and Ross – support me in that. What more could I wish for?

I grew up with Thai cuisine. As a young girl, growing up in Thailand, I used to make the charcoal with my grandma and learn how to make pastes. In Thailand, we learned that food was a way of communicating. We learned to give; we'd show our respect to the village monks by giving them food.

Each morning, at 6am, the village bell would ring and we'd prepare food for the

about suree

monks who were walking to the temple. Monks don't eat after noon (it's part of their Buddhist religion) so we would feed them early in the day.

I grew up in Pa Ya Man, near northern Thailand, with my grandma, who taught me how to cook. Cooking was a very communal experience. It's something that all of us did together. We'd spend hours cooking with other families and women in the village. It was a way of bringing the community together; it made us close-knit. I learned how to cook pastes and sauces and I still use the recipes that I learned then to this day. That's why my food tastes authentic: I'm using many of the recipes that I used as a five-year-old girl learning at the knee of my grandma.

I came to the UK when I was 21, so that I could study at college. I ran my own business, which involved printing business cards and handing them out door to door. For a while, I worked in the rag trade, making clothes. I'd also cook for my friends – and they'd all be blown away. They started to book me and soon I was cooking four-course meals for 20 people at a time.

When I met Simon, my husband, his family helped me to open my own restaurant: I've never looked back.

It's an exhausting profession, but I love it very much. Our first restaurant was at Ironbridge, in Shropshire, and we were there for eight-and-a-half years. Then we moved to nearby Broseley in 2008.

I enjoyed great fortune in 2012 when I was named the best Thai chef in the UK. Winning the 2012 Thai Chef of the Year for the whole of the British Isles was a remarkable achievement. I was up against some of the biggest stars in British cuisine – and I won. My success was down to one simple ingredient: authenticity. Though I like to play with presentation and make my food as pretty and artistic as can be, the flavours that my guests taste are the same as those that I first cooked back in Thailand.

Every night, people will find me at the stove of The King and Thai, in Broseley. I'm ever-present; I'm not the sort of chef who flies the nest to do personal appearances or star turns elsewhere. When people come to my restaurant they know exactly who'll be cooking their food: me.

My passion for Thai cuisine has never dimmed. It's my way of sharing my culture. Thai food is the freshest in the world. It's healthy, it's about great flavour and it's about being creative and daring.

I sincerely hope you enjoy my recipes. I'm sharing with you the food of my childhood and my life. It's yours to adapt, enjoy and eat. I hope you relish every mouthful.

Suree

ingredients

Building a store cupboard of ingredients is essential for Thai cooks. We rely on the freshest herbs, augmented with a little spice, so you need to have easy access to supplies. Most supermarkets now stock the essentials, such as lemongrass, ginger, garlic and coriander. You'll also find it relatively easy to pick up fresh chillies and spices including cumin, coriander seed, cloves and star anise.

Other ingredients may be a little harder to find. But persevere and you'll find stocks of tamarind, shrimp paste, galangal and lesser galangal in specialist shops or through online suppliers. You may also be able to find ingredients such as fresh turmeric root. It's worth the extra effort. Fresh ingredients pack a far more powerful flavour than their dry or powdered counterparts.

Store cupboard ingredients tend to be used for making the pastes that are at the heart of Thai cooking. You'll need galangal and lemongrass, for instance, to make a variety of different dishes.

There is a golden rule that applies to Thai cooking and it is this: the freshest ingredients will give you the best results. So go the extra mile to find a good stockist, whether that's a local shop or a great online trader. You'll be glad that you did.

As well as herbs, roots, stalks and leaves, you'll also need a good supply of sauces, oils, sugars and creams.

Thai cooking relies on such ingredients. Coconut cream is a richer version of coconut milk and is available in most supermarkets. You'll also rely on different types of soy sauce. Light soy sauce is lighter in flavour than the more deeply flavoured and richer dark variety. Both are readily available, as is sesame oil. You should also find it fairly straightforward to track down fish sauce and oyster sauce.

Finally, it's worth stocking up on palm sugar. Palm sugar comes from the palm tree, while cane sugar comes from sugar cane. There are subtle differences between the two, though if you're unable to find palm sugar, go ahead and use normal granulated varieties.

Ingredients

Whatever ingredients you are using, be willing to experiment a little. My recipes will give you great results, but don't be afraid to add a little more chilli, for instance, if you like your food hot; or a little extra coconut cream, if you like it mild and creamy. Here's a quick run-down of what ingredients bring to your pastes and sauces.

HERBS AND SPICES

- **Cardamom**. The world's third most expensive spice, behind saffron and vanilla, has an intensely aromatic, slightly sweet flavour. My recipes use green cardamom, rather than black.
- **Chillies**. Give you added kick. I use dried red, and large fresh red or green.
- **Cinnamom**. Use bark, if you can find it, but powdered is also fine.
- **Cloves**. Use sparsely, as they have a strong flavour. Pairs well with cinnamon, allspice and basil.
- **Coriander**. The leaves have herby, citrus overtones.
- **Coriander seed**. For lemony, citrus flavour.
- **Cumin**. Distinctive aroma and adds earthy, warming feeling to a dish.
- **Galangal**. Has a distinct peppery cinnamon flavour.
- **Ginger**. Amazing flavour and therapeutic effects.
- **Lemongrass**. It has a sweet, lemon taste.
- **Lesser galangal**. This has a sharper, hotter, stronger and more medicinal taste than galangal.
- **Shrimp paste**. A compelling, salty taste.
- **Star anise**. Liquorice-like aroma; it enhances the flavour of meat.
- **Tamarind**. A sweet-and-sour taste.
- **Turmeric**. Earthy, like horseradish or mustard.

SAUCES, OILS AND SUGAR

- **Coconut cream and coconut milk**. Creamy, slightly nutty and mild.
- **Fish sauce**. Imparts umami flavour. Used as a condiment to season and enhance many dishes.
- **Oyster sauce**. Savoury taste that enhances flavour.
- **Palm sugar**. Has a far superior taste to regular sugar. Not as sickly sweet.
- **Sesame oil** – Pure sesame oil is best, and has a mild sesame taste. Its nutty overtones enhance a dish.
- **Soy sauce (light)**. Saltier and savoury.
- **Soy sauce (dark)**. Darker, richer, more full-bodied and slightly sweeter than its light counterpart.

sauces/pastes

Sauces and pastes are the basis of all good Thai cuisine. Pastes provide a real taste explosion and are the building blocks for curries, soups and a range of other dishes. In this section, I look at some of my favourite sauces, pastes and marinades, explaining how to make them. Some, like satay and sweet chilli, can be used as dipping sauces; others, like the famous green and red curry pastes, are the cornerstone of dishes. The ten sauces that follow are essentials for any aspiring Thai cook. There are many more, of course, but if you can master these, you've every chance of culinary success.

SATAY DIP

This satay sauce can be served with chicken, pork or beef, on skewers.

INGREDIENTS
2 or 3 dried chillies
5 shallots
10 cloves of garlic
1 tsp galangal, chopped
1 tsp lemongrass, chopped
2 kaffir lime leaves
1 tsp coriander seed
1 tsp cumin seed
1 tsp shrimp paste
1 tbsp sugar, to taste
1 tsp rice wine vinegar, to taste
Pinch of sea salt, to taste
100g roasted peanuts
1 tin coconut cream (approx 400ml)
2 tbsp cooking oil

METHOD
● Pan roast or roast the chillies, chopped galangal, shallots, garlic, coriander and cumin seed for five minutes at around 180C, until the aromas are released. You're looking to roast – not burn – the ingredients, to bring out the maximum flavour.
● Now take a pestle and mortar and grind together the pan-roasted ingredients, along with the lemongrass, kaffir lime leaves and shrimp paste.
● Pour the cooking oil into a pan and gently fry the paste for around five minutes. Pour in the coconut cream and set aside.
● Now grind the peanuts and add them to the cream paste. Add the sugar, rice wine vinegar and salt and simmer for 15 minutes, until the sauce thickens. Make sure you continually stir to prevent the mixture from burning on the bottom of the pan.

sauces/pastes

SWEET CHILLI DIP

I love making Thai sweet chilli dip. It's so versatile: you can use it as a sauce, marinade or dip. It's wonderfully healthy and works as a condiment for many dishes. I like to pair it with chicken or fish, as well as other seafood. You can use it on the grill, or as a dip for finger foods. In the restaurant, we serve it with starter platters, so diners can use it to add sweet, piquant heat to spring rolls, prawn toasts and other appetisers.

INGREDIENTS

10 large fresh red chillies, very finely chopped
5 cloves of garlic, very finely chopped
100g sugar
50g rice wine vinegar
1 tbsp salt

METHOD

● In a large pan, gently cook the sugar with the rice wine vinegar until you form a syrup. Add the salt and stir, so that it dissolves.

● Now incorporate the chillies and garlic and cook through. Simmer for around 20 minutes, so that the chillies and garlic almost dissolve.

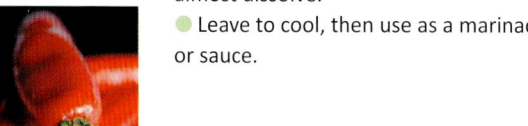

● Leave to cool, then use as a marinade or sauce.

CUCUMBER VINAIGRETTE

This simple vinaigrette is Thai cooking at its best. It brings together delicious, complementary flavours: cool with hot, spicy with sweet. I recommend it with vegetable fritters or fish cakes.

INGREDIENTS
100g sugar
60ml rice wine vinegar
1 tsp salt
½ cucumber, thinly sliced
2 shallots, sliced
1 fresh red chilli, sliced
½ small carrot, thinly sliced

METHOD
- Mix together the sugar, vinegar and salt in a pan. Bring to the boil and then remove from the heat. Leave to cool.
- Once cool, add the sliced shallots, cucumber, chilli and carrot. Leave to pickle for between 30 minutes and an hour, then serve.

sauces/pastes

SWEET-AND-SOUR SAUCE

This recipe for sweet-and-sour sauce is easy and goes brilliantly with chicken, pork or tofu dishes. It can also be used as a dip. It has a wonderful tang and can be made as spicy or as mild as you wish. Once you've made your own Thai sweet-and-sour sauce, you'll never buy a shop-sold sauce again. It's delicious.

INGREDIENTS
200g sugar
120ml rice wine vinegar
1 tsp salt
2 tbsp tomato purée
2 tbsp tomato ketchup
225g pineapple
125g water
1 stem fresh ginger

METHOD
● Mix together all of the ingredients in a pan and bring to the boil. Cook until the sugar is absorbed by the liquid.
● Leave to simmer for around 30 minutes, until the pineapple disintegrates and the sauce becomes thick and sticky. Serve hot or cool.

RED CURRY PASTE

Red curry and green curry are synonymous with Thai cooking. Thai curries differ significantly from curries made in other parts of south Asia and are characterised by their use of fresh ingredients, including herbs and aromatic leaves, rather than a spice blend. The heat is determined by the amount of chilli used in the paste, so if you prefer it mild use less and if you prefer it hot use more.

INGREDIENTS

1 tsp chopped galangal
2 tbsp chopped lemongrass
2 tbsp chopped shallots
1 tsp garlic
1 tsp shrimp paste
5 dried chillies, though you can use fresh chillies
1 tsp sea salt
2 kaffir lime leaves

METHOD

- Use a pestle and mortar to pound all of the ingredients together. Blend until the paste is fine and you have eliminated any of the long fibres of the lemongrass.
- You can stir fry the paste in cooking oil before adding other ingredients to the dish. The oil reaches a much higher temperature than boiling water, which releases unique flavours from the ingredients in the paste.

sauces/pastes

GREEN CURRY PASTE

Markets in Thailand sell incredible curry pastes of all colours and flavours. They make for an incredible sight, with ladies sat around huge stainless steels. The pastes are ladled out for customers.

INGREDIENTS

1 tsp galangal
2 tsp lemongrass
2 tsp finely chopped shallots
4 cloves garlic
2 kaffir lime leaves
1 tsp sea salt
1 tsp black pepper
1 tsp coriander seeds
1 tsp cumin seeds
½ tsp shrimp paste (omit this, if making the sauce for vegetarians)
4 large green chillies

METHOD

- Pan roast or roast the cumin seeds and coriander seeds at 180C for five minutes, so as to release the natural flavours.
- Now grind all ingredients to a fine paste using a pestle and mortar. As with the red curry paste, the mixture can be stir-fried in cooking oil to release additional flavour before being used.

MASSAMAN CURRY PASTE

Massaman curry is thought to have originated in central Thailand during the 16th century, though there are many differing theories as to how it was created. The dish has Muslim roots and is most commonly made with beef, though its robust flavours mean it also works well with duck, tofu, chicken, or, for non-Muslims, with pork. Massaman is one of the richest and most flavoursome dishes in the world. Served with meltingly tender beef, it's curry heaven.

INGREDIENTS

10 large dried chillies, soaked in water so as to soften
1 tbsp galangal
2 tbsp shallot
1 tbsp lemongrass
6–8 garlic cloves
1 tsp cumin seed
1 tsp coriander seed
1 tsp shrimp paste
1 tsp sea salt
2 tbsp tamarind paste
1 tbsp palm sugar (you can substitute granulated sugar)

METHOD

- Pan roast or roast the galangal, shallot, garlic, cumin seed and coriander seed at 180C for about five minutes, to release the flavours.
- Now pound all of the ingredients together into a fine paste.
- As with the green and red curries, you may decide to stir fry the paste over a high heat with a little cooking oil, so as to extract even more flavour.

sauces/pastes

PANANG CURRY PASTE

Panang curry paste is generally milder than most other Thai curries. Often, panang curries do not contain vegetables but use only meat. Beef panang is particularly popular, though vegetarians can also enjoy the dish by substituting the beef for tofu.

INGREDIENTS

6 shallots, chopped
2 bulbs of garlic
1 tbsp galangal
1 tsp coriander seed
1 tsp cumin seed
1 tsp peppercorns
2 stalks lemongrass
2 kaffir lime leaves
1 tsp shrimp paste
1 tsp sea salt
8 large dried chillies

METHOD

- Soak the chillies in water until soft.
- Pan-roast or roast the coriander seed and cumin seed at 180C for five minutes, until the aromas are released.
- Now pound together all of the ingredients and mash to a fine paste using a pestle and mortar. Stir-frying in hot oil will enhance the flavour.

YELLOW CURRY PASTE

Yellow curry is probably the richest and creamiest of the Thai curries. The paste is added to coconut cream and milk, when cooked, which gives it a mild taste. It is particularly popular in Western countries.

INGREDIENTS

6 dried red chillies, soaked in water until soft
4 shallots
5 cloves of garlic
1 tbsp lemongrass
1 tsp cumin seed
1 tsp coriander seed
1 tsp fresh turmeric (you can use turmeric powder, if you are unable to obtain fresh supplies)
1 tsp sea salt
½ tsp shrimp paste
½ tsp ground cinnamon
1 tsp galangal

METHOD

- Pan roast or roast the cumin and coriander seeds for around five minutes at 180C so as to release the flavours.
- Now grind ingredients together in a pestle and mortar.
- The paste can be stir-fried before use in hot oil, so as to release maximum flavour.

24   COOK THAI WITH SUREE COATES

sauces/pastes

SOUR CURRY

Sour curry is particularly popular in Southern Thailand and has a spicier, sharper taste than yellow curry.

Shrimp paste is a key ingredient in this dish. It is possible to make it, but the process takes a very long time. For the best results, buy a tub of shrimp paste from your local Chinese supermarket or specialist deli, or from online outlets.

INGREDIENTS

12 dried large chillies, soaked in water to soften
2 roots of lesser galangal
6 shallots
1 tbsp lemongrass, chopped
½ tsp shrimp paste

METHOD

- Pound all of the ingredients in a pestle and mortar to a fine paste. Stir fry in hot oil to release extra flavour.

25

SPICY KING PRAWN SOUP

soups

Tom Yam Goong – the Thai name for this dish – is the king of Thai soups. The word 'Tom' refers to the boiling process and the word 'Yam' indicates a spicy and sour dish. The dish is loved throughout South East Asia and is made with fragrant herbs. Prawns are often the main ingredient, though there are similar soups that feature mixed seafood or chicken. This is a brilliantly simple dish to make; the secret is to find the freshest possible ingredients for the paste, so as to extract maximum flavour.

INGREDIENTS

3 thin shoots of galangal, finely sliced
2 stalks lemongrass
2 shallots, crushed
500ml chicken stock
1 tbsp fish sauce, to taste
1 tbsp lime juice, to taste
½ a bird's-eye chilli
1 tsp sugar, to taste
3 or 4 kaffir lime leaves
12 large prawns
A generous handful of mushrooms
125ml coconut cream
A handful of chopped coriander
A pinch of salt, to taste

METHOD

● Clean the prawns by taking off their heads, shelling the body and removing the internal tract – the long, thin dark-coloured vein that runs from top to tail. Set aside.
● Make the Tom Yam paste: cut the lemongrass into 1cm pieces and add to the galangal, shallots, kaffir lime leaves, chilli and salt. Blitz or grind together to a paste. Transfer to a heavy-bottomed pan and add the chicken stock. Cook over a medium-high heat and bring to the boil.
● Now add the prawns. When the prawns begin to turn pink, add the mushrooms and cook for a further two minutes. Turn off the heat.
● Add the fish sauce, lime juice, sugar and coconut cream. Adjust the seasoning to suit.
● Add a handful of chopped coriander and serve in bowls.

SPICY CHICKEN SOUP

This is the chicken version of Tom Yam Goong (see page 26). It is simple to make and incredibly tasty. It can be served as an appetiser or as the star player. It is particular popular during the cooler months of autumn and winter, because it has such a warm and spicy flavour, and a wonderful balance of spicy, salty, sweet and sour flavours.

INGREDIENTS

2 shallots, crushed
2 lemongrass stalks, cut into 2cm pieces
4 thin shoots of galangal, finely sliced
300ml coconut cream
1,500ml chicken stock
2 chicken breasts, cut into thin strips
3 or 4 kaffir lime leaves
1 tbsp lemon juice
½ tbsp sugar
1 tbsp fish sauce
A handful of chopped coriander and spring onion

OPTIONAL EXTRAS

You can also add a handful of mushrooms, throwing them into the soup to cook through during the last three minutes.
Garnish: Thin, curly ribbons of radish can also add a delightful flourish.

METHOD

- This is very similar to the method for Spicy King Prawn Soup. Blitz the lower portion of the lemongrass stalk, though the upper portion will be fine in stalks. Place the shallots, lemongrass, lime leaves and galangal into a heavy-bottomed pan.
- Pour in the coconut cream and chicken stock. Cook over a medium-high heat and bring to the boil.
- Add the chicken strips and cook through. Now add mushrooms (if you are using them), lemon juice, sugar and fish sauce.
- Take off the heat and adjust the seasoning. If you like your soup hot, add further chilli; if you like it mild, add a little more coconut cream. You're looking to achieve a balance of flavour – you want to be able to taste the spicy, sour, salty and sweet elements. They should complement one another, not drown each other out.
- Sprinkle with a handful of chopped coriander and spring onion.

CHEF'S TIP: This dish also works well with noodles, though always add the noodles to the dish after the soup is cooked. If you add the noodles while the dish is cooking, the soup will become 'gloopy' because of the addition of starch.

NOODLE SOUP WITH MINCED PORK BALLS

soups

This is a highly popular dish that is packed with wonderful flavours. Like most Thai soups, you'll find it wonderfully fresh and nourishing. As well as tasting great, Thai soups are also great at chasing away colds and flus, because they are packed with vitamins and the heat from herbs and spices. The texture of the pork and noodles is a wonderful contrast to the clear, silky broth.

INGREDIENTS

250g pork, minced
50g rice noodle, soaked in water until soft
1 clove of garlic, crushed, plus 1 separate clove of sliced garlic
½ tsp ground black pepper
850ml pork stock or chicken stock
⅔ tbsp fish sauce
2 tbsp cooking oil
Spring onion and coriander, chopped coarsely to finish

METHOD

● Add the black pepper and clove of crushed garlic to the minced pork. Add the fish sauce, mix well and set aside to marinate.

● Make garlic oil by finely chopping the other bulb of garlic and adding to the oil. Pour into a pan and cook through, until the garlic starts to lightly brown. Take off the heat immediately, to stop from burning. (If you leave it for too long, the garlic will burn and create a bitter taste.) Set aside to cool.

● Pour the stock into a saucepan. Bring to near boiling point then turn down the heat.

● Roll out the pork into small balls in your hand. Now add them to the hot stock. When the pork balls are cooked, add more fish sauce, to taste.

● Take off the heat and add in a small amount of garlic oil, to taste. Add the noodles, to warm through, then serve, garnishing with chopped coriander and spring onion.

starters

Prawn toasts are a perennial favourite. They are popular around the world, from Australia, throughout Asia and into Europe and North America. There are numerous recipes, some using egg, though I prefer to keep mine simple, so as to extract maximum flavour. Using minced prawns is the key to this recipe. They stick together, almost like glue, so you don't really need to use a binding agent.

It's not just about creating delicious starters, of course. I also like to make sure there are great garnishes and dips. Be creative and use your imagination. By doing so, you'll be able to convert a simple starter into a sensational starter.

INGREDIENTS
250g raw prawn (shelled, de-veined)
4 slices bread
125g sesame seeds
Pinch of salt
Pinch of ground black pepper
Cooking oil for deep frying
Cucumber vinaigrette (see page 18)

METHOD
- Mince the prawns and season with salt and pepper, then put to one side.
- Slice the bread into triangles. Spread the seasoned prawn paste onto the toast, then sprinkle with sesame seeds until they are completely covered.
- Deep fry until golden brown in oil that is heated to around 170C – it should take between five and six minutes.
- Serve with cucumber vinaigrette.

GARNISH
I like to garnish my prawn toasts with cucumber and carrot curls. Simply take half a cucumber and a single carrot and finely slice them on a mandoline. Now wrap the slices of carrot and cucumber around your finger at the same time, so that they are interwoven. Stand up on end, like soldiers.

TEMPURA VEGETABLE WITH CUCUMBER VINAIGRETTE

starters

I like to stack my vegetable tempura high in a bowl and decorate them with edible flowers and small shoots of coriander. You can also make a small mango salsa (using tiny dice of peppers, chilli and mango) which adds flavour, spice and colour, as well as a little texture. In many ways, this dish is the essence of Thai cooking: it uses the freshest ingredients, it takes just a few minutes to cook, and the effect is absolutely stunning.

INGREDIENTS

250g vegetables – eg sweet potatos, carrots, parsnips. Feel free to use your imagination – you can use French beans, mangetouts, broccoli, red onions or any vegetable of your choice.

FOR TEMPURA BATTER MIX:
150g plain flour (to cater for wheat- and gluten-intolerance you can use rice flour or '00' flour – if doing so, you must add in one tsp of cornflour)
Pinch of salt
1 tsp ground black pepper
120ml sparkling water or soda water

METHOD

- First, make the batter. Add the water to the flour and seasoning, and mix thoroughly until all is incorporated. The consistency should be like a pancake mix and there should be no lumps.
- Thinly slice the vegetables into strips. Dip them into the batter and deep fry in oil heated to 170C. They should emerge from the fryer golden brown and crisp, which should take about five minutes.

CALAMARI

starters

Calamari is a dish popular in Mediterranean cuisine. It's just as popular in Thai cuisine. Squid is eaten throughout Asia, including Japan – which eats a staggering 700,000 tons each year. In other parts of the world, like Australia, New Zealand and South Africa, calamari is even eaten in fish-and-chip shops. The key to this dish is to buy the freshest ingredients, make sure everything is clean and then avoid overcooking the squid.

This is the simplest recipe ever. It's a treat, something quick and easy and yummy.

INGREDIENTS

2 × squid (cleaned), cut it into strips or tubes, whichever you prefer, make sure they are no more than 1cm thick
100g plain flour
Pinch of salt
Pinch of black pepper

METHOD

● Coat the squid in the seasoned flour and deep fry at around 170C for two minutes. You don't want to overcook the calamari, otherwise it will become tough and rubbery. If you want to add variety, you can also add in squid tentacles.

● Garnish with thin slices of lime or lemon, juicy vine-ripened tomatoes and a bed of shredded lettuce. I like to serve it with a sweet chilli dip.

VEGETABLE SAMOSA WITH MANGO SALAD

starters

INGREDIENTS

250g root vegetables – potato, carrot, sweet potato, parsnip. Feel free to use others
A handful of coriander
Pinch of black pepper
Pinch of sea salt
½ tsp vegetable stock – approx 20g
8 sheets filo pastry
1 egg to brush the pastry and seal
1 tsp medium curry powder. If you like it hot, put more, or use hot curry powder rather than medium
Pinch of sugar
1 clove garlic
1 medium onion
Cooking oil

For the mango salsa
1 ripe mango, cut into 1cm dice
1 red onion, cut into small dice
1 large red chilli, cut into very fine dice
1 squeeze lemon juice

METHOD

● Combine all of the salsa ingredients and leave to stand for an hour, so that the flavours infuse.
● Begin to make your samosas by dicing all the vegetable into 1cm cubes, crush the garlic and slice the onion.
● Stir fry the garlic and onion. Now add in all the root vegetables and the vegetable stock. Cook slowly until all of the vegetables are soft and tender, but still have bite. The texture should be al dente, similar to pasta or rice in Italian cuisine.
● Season with curry powder and salt and pepper, as well as the sugar. Remove from the heat and leave to cool.
● Sprinkle with chopped coriander once cool – if you do this while the coriander is still warm it will wilt and discolour.
● Take the filo pastry and cut into long strips. The size of these will depend upon how large you'd like your samosas. If you want small ones, use 5cm, if you want large, use 10cm strips. Cover with a damp tea towel to prevent drying.
● Put the samosa mix onto the pastry strips and fold over into a triangle. Brush the edges with egg wash to seal, then plunge into the deep fat fryer. Cook for about five minutes at 170C until golden brown.
● Drain, then serve as shown.

SPRING ROLLS

starters

Spring rolls are ubiquitous in Thailand. They can be filled with a variety of fillings, including meat, chicken, fish, shellfish and vegetables or tofu. The cooking technique and fillings vary considerably across Thailand.

Spring rolls are brimful of flavour. There are fried and non-fried versions. I like them fried because the end result has a delicious hot, crunchy texture.

INGREDIENTS
8 sheets of spring roll skin (you can buy from oriental stores)
100g beansprouts
100g grated carrot
100g grated cabbage
50g coriander, finely chopped
Pinch of sea salt
20ml vegetable stock
Pinch of sugar
1 bundle (about 25g) vermicelli rice noodle, soaked in hot water for five minutes until soft

METHOD
- Stir-fry all the vegetables together in hot oil and seasoning. When cooked, add the softened noodles and adjust seasoning.
- Leave to cool then sprinkle with coriander.
- Wrap in the spring roll skins and fold over the ends, so that the filling does not escape.
- Deep fry in oil at 170C until they are golden brown. This should take no more than five minutes.
- Serve with sweet chilli sauce.

TO GARNISH
Spring rolls can be served in a variety of ways. You can serve them as a stack, so that your guests can simply tuck in and help themselves, dipping the rolls into a sweet chilli dip. You can alternatively cut them diagonally across the centre, and serve them in small edible baskets. If you want to decorate the plate, you can garnish with a little mango salsa, made from finely diced mango, chilli and pepper.

CHICKEN SATAY

starters

Satay is extremely popular and can be made with a variety of different ingredients, including chicken, goat, beef, fish, tofu, pork and shellfish. It originated in Indonesia but is popular throughout Thailand. It's available from many street markets, travelling street vendors and restaurants – little wonder it was voted by CNN as one of the world's most popular foods.

When making satay, people in Thailand often use skewers from the midrib of the coconut palm frond. That's not possible in other parts of the world, including the UK, so people favour short skewers. My top tip is to dip those skewers in water for at least half an hour before cooking the satay, otherwise the skewers will burn and the satay will be impossible to eat.

INGREDIENTS

250g breast chicken meat, sliced into thin strips. Slicing the chicken helps when the chicken is immersed in the marinade; it has a greater surface area and can absorb more of the flavours

FOR THE MARINADE
1 tsp galangal
1 tsp fresh ginger
3 stems lemongrass
4 kaffir lime leaves
1 tbsp turmeric powder
Pinch of salt
1 tbsp honey
150ml coconut cream

METHOD

● Blend the marinade ingredients together and cover the chicken strips with them. Set aside for 30 minutes, so that the meat can absorb the flavours. You can leave the chicken strips in the marinade for much longer if you want them to have a stronger flavour.

● Put the chicken (or other meats) onto the skewers and barbecue them, or griddle them on a hot pan, until cooked through. It's ideal if you can get chargrill marks across them because they add flavour.

● Serve with satay sauce (see page 16).

PORK DUMPLING WITH A DIPPING SAUCE

starters

Dumplings are delicious. They are popularly served in dim sum. The range of fillings and flavourings is completely up to you: minced lamb, pork, whole or chopped prawns, mushrooms and crabmeat all make amazing fillings. They are delicious served with a dipping sauce.

INGREDIENTS

200g minced pork
20g raw prawn (cleaned, shell-removed and deveined)
Pinch of sea salt
1 tsp light soy sauce
Pinch of black pepper
12 sheets won ton pastry
1 egg, whisked

FOR THE DIPPING SAUCE
Light soy sauce
1 lemon
1 red chilli, finely chopped

METHOD

- Mince the cleaned prawns and add them to the pork. Add all the other dumpling ingredients and mix together.
- Roll the minced ingredients into small balls. I like to do that by squeezing some mix through my hand, then scooping off a teaspoonful.
- Put each ball into the centre of a sheet of pastry and wrap the pastry around it, leaving a small 'bunch' at the top, which can be sealed with a little beaten egg.
- Steam for 15 minutes.
- For the dipping sauce, combine the soy sauce with a squeeze of lemon juice and the chilli. Adjust the seasoning to taste.

LEMON CHICKEN

starters

This is a light, fragrant and refreshing dish. The marinade for the chicken brings out a lot of amazing flavours – it really is a treat. As with all Thai cooking, the secret is to use the freshest possible ingredients. The fresher the ingredients, the fuller the flavours.

INGREDIENTS

3 chicken breasts, minced
3 stems lemongrass, finely sliced
5 shallots, finely sliced
4 spring onions, finely chopped
A handful of coriander, finely chopped
Pinch of sugar
1 tbsp fish sauce
1 tsp chilli powder
1 tsp lemon juice
8 lettuce leaves, to wrap the chicken in

METHOD

● Put about four tablespoons of water into a pan over a medium heat. Add all of the ingredients, except for the lettuce. Adjust seasoning to taste.

● Leave to cool, then serve in lettuce leaves. You can garnish with extra spring onion.

FISH CAKES

starters

Recipes for fish cakes vary around the world. In England, they tend to feature plenty of potato, which makes them a meal in themselves. I prefer the Thai version. They use prawn and fish, plus seasonings, which makes them deliciously light and fluffy. The absence of potato means they are not quite as filling – so you can eat an extra one. The minced prawn helps to bind the ingredients together; it acts almost like glue.

INGREDIENTS

400g white fish, such as cod or haddock
150g raw prawn (cleaned, shelled and deveined)
1 tbsp red curry paste
2 kaffir lime leaves, finely sliced
A handful of sliced French beans
1 tbsp fish sauce
Pinch of sugar
1 egg, beaten

METHOD

- Mince the fish and prawns together, until they are soft and gooey. Now add the beaten egg and combine. Season with all of the other ingredients.
- Shape into cakes and deep fry until golden brown. That should take about six to eight minutes, at 170C.
- Serve with cucumber vinaigrette (see page 18).

SPICY BEEF SALAD

starters

This light, aromatic salad packs a flavour punch. The beef gives it body and depth while the delicious marinades bring balance and excitement to the dish. It's a delicious looking salad, I think, and I like to garnish it with mint leaves, sliced spring onion, onion rings and micro salad leaves. I also add a few sunblush tomatoes, for extra flavour and colour. The salad recipe remains the same, however you want to present it. Use your imagination and combine the best seasonal ingredients.

When selecting your beef, choose between rump and fillet. Rump has more taste, so that would be my preference, but some people like the tenderness of fillet.

INGREDIENTS

275g rump or fillet steak
1 tsp chilli powder
2 tsp fish sauce
2 tsp lemon juice
1 pinch of sugar
1 handful of fresh mint leaves
1 handful of coriander leaves

METHOD

● Season the steak and sear in a hot pan, so that it's completed sealed. Now cook for two minutes, then turn and cook the other side for a further 90 seconds, if you want rare. For medium, it's three minutes, then two-and-a-half. For well done, it's four minutes, then three-and-a-half. Cooking times will vary according to the thickness and shape of the meat, so these instructions only ever serve as a guide. Once you've cooked the meat, allow it to rest for a few minutes, so that the fibres relax and it becomes more tender. Then finely slice it.

● Now make the sauce by combining the chilli powder, fish sauce, lemon juice and sugar. Simply mix together and drizzle over the meat.

● To serve, sprinkle chopped mint and coriander onto the plate and place the slices of beef on top, adding tomatoes, spring onions or whatever you choose.

MUSSELS

starters

I'm a big fan of shellfish. I love it's freshness and lightness. Adding fragrant Thai ingredients, like lemongrass and chilli, really helps to enhance the flavour. Thai versions of mussels are much less filling than European dishes, which rely heavily on cream and wine. I think this dish is an absolute treat, and it's so easy.

INGREDIENTS

1 family bag of mussels, clean with beards removed
5 chopped shallots
1 clove garlic
2 stems lemongrass, crushed then cut into 1cm pieces– it's not for eating, just for flavour
1 red chilli, sliced
200ml coconut cream
fish sauce
1 lemon, juiced
1 tbsp sugar

METHOD

● In a pan, put a tablespoon of cooking oil. Stir-fry the garlic, lemongrass, chilli and shallots until soft.

● Put in the mussels, add the coconut cream and cook for two minutes until the mussel shells start to open. Throw away any mussels that have not opened.

● Season with fish sauce, lemon juice and sugar – after the mussels have opened, so the flavours go in and season the tender, golden flesh.

● Keep tasting and season accordingly.
You are looking for a hot, sweet and sour combination.

fish

SEA BREAM AND ASPARAGUS

fish

This is a delightful dish that combines fish, a vegetable-filled samosa and seasonal vegetables. I like to serve it with asparagus, but you could substitute that for an alternative, such as fine beans, if they are in season. I add swishes of red curry sauce, to give the dish extra flavour, and then garnish with celeriac crisps, which are deep-fried. There's a wonderful combination of texture, with the crunch of the samosa and crisps and the soft, delicate textures of the vegetables and fish. The flavours are also well balanced, with sweet spicy hints from the sauce and delicate salty flavours from the sea bream. It's a quick dish to make and the results are stunning.

INGREDIENTS

4 sea bream fillets
1 bunch asparagus
Grated celeriac
4 radishes
2 tbsp red curry sauce
1 tbsp oil
Vegetable samosa (see page 38)
Dill to garnish

METHOD

- Make the samosa and set aside.
- Add the oil to a hot pan and fry the four sea bream fillets. Fry skin side down for a couple of minutes, until golden brown and crisp, then turn over.
- At the same time and in a separate pan, blanch the asparagus for two minutes in salted boiling water.
- Assemble as shown, with swishes of red curry sauce for colour, contrast and flavour. Garnish with dill and celeriac crisps, which are made by deep-frying celeriac that has been grated through a thick aperture.

WRAPPED SOLE WITH ASPARAGUS, MUSHROOMS AND COCONUT-AND-LEMONGRASS SAUCE

fish

One of the most beautiful aspects of Thai cooking is the lightness of dishes. This is a perfect example. Tender pak choi, asparagus and tiny hon-shimeji mushrooms add subtle flavour to the delicate sole fillets. A little red chilli adds heat, as do the black peppercorns, while the coconut sauce adds a satisfying richness, without overpowering the other ingredients. It's a delightfully appetising dish that is extremely healthy.

INGREDIENTS
4 sole fillets
1 bunch of asparagus
2 pak choi
1 red chilli
1 packet of oriental mushrooms (I like hon-shimeji)
400ml coconut cream
1 handful chopped coriander
1 thumb-sized stalk of ginger
Juice of 1 lemon
1 stalk lemongrass
4 slices galangal
1 tbsp fish sauce
Pinch of sugar
Pinch of rock salt
Pinch of black peppercorns

METHOD
- First, make the sauce. Add the coconut cream, lemon juice, galangal, sugar, fish sauce and lemongrass to a heavy-bottomed pan and bring to a boil. Take off the heat and allow the flavours to infuse.
- Sprinkle the sole fillets with the sea salt and black peppercorns. Roll and wrap in cling film, then steam for around 12 minutes in the cling film, until cooked through. Rest.
- Make ginger crisps, for garnish, by finely grating the ginger and then deep-frying until golden brown.
- Cook the pak choi in boiling water for two minutes. Cook the asparagus in the same way. Blanch the mushrooms in boiling water for a minute.
- Assembly by pouring the sauce into the bowl and adding the mushrooms, pak choi and asparagus. Now sit the fish on top and then garnish with the ginger crisps.

SEA BASS WITH POTATO GALETTE AND WILD BLACK COCONUT RICE

fish

This is a stunning dish which provides wonderful contrasts of colour, texture and taste. The cone of wild black coconut rice adds a flourish to the dish, while the potato galette, which is cooked at the same time as the fish, gives it a classy edge. Drops of sauce and small slivers of chilli, together with opened clams, complete a stunning picture. I love to make my food look pretty and this is a dish that scores extra points on that front. I garnish this dish with wild black fennel, though you can substitute other herbs if you wish.

INGREDIENTS

4 sea bass fillets, skin on
250g wild black rice
400ml coconut milk
Handful desiccated coconut
250g Charlotte (or other waxy) potatoes
12 clams
1 large red chilli
2 tbsp oil
1 thumb-sized root of ginger
2 tbsp light soy sauce
Juice of half a lemon
Pinch of sugar
Pinch of salt
4 pak choi
1 banana leaf
Black fennel, to garnish

METHOD

● Cut the banana leaf into four equal pieces and roll each into a cone. Divide the wild black rice between the cones and add the coconut milk. Season with a pinch of salt. Close the cones, so that the liquid cannot escape. Place inside a steamer and steam for at least one-and-a-half hours, so that the rice is sticky and the liquid absorbed. When you remove it from the cone, it will retain its cone shape. Dress with a handful of desiccated coconut.

● For the clams, add a tablespoon of oil into a wok and heat until smoking hot. Add four clams per person. Add a little sliced ginger and sliced red chilli. Now add the soy sauce, a pinch of sugar and the lemon juice. Cook quickly. Discard any clams that do not open. Reserve the cooking liquor to use on your plate as a dressing.

● Take the pak choi and blanch for two minutes in hot water. Roll and place on the plate. Serve straight away.

● Season the sea bass fillets with salt and pepper. Cut the potatoes, using a mandoline, then create the galette by layering them on the skin side of the fish. Add a tablespoon of oil to a pan and heat until smoking hot. Add the fish to the pan, galette side down. Do this gently, so that the galette does not fall from the fish. Cook for two minutes, to get a golden colour. Carefully lift up the fish and cook the other side on a lower heat until the fish is cooked through. Assemble as shown and dress with a little black fennel, or a similar herb.

SALMON TERIYAKI WITH WILD-HERB SALAD AND VEGETABLE BATONS

This is a beautiful dish that is surprisingly simple. It's a dish that packs a flavoursome punch – and in terms of presentation it has a real 'wow factor'. I like to cook my salmon on a chargrill, to give it wonderful criss-cross marks across the flesh. The golden teriyaki sauce gives it a burnished-gold colour while the addition of a sliced radish, wild chive flowers and a 'cube' of vegetable batons makes it look absolutely stunning. It's the sort of dish that you'd expect in a Michelin-starred restaurant – but you'll find you're able to make it in the comfort of your own kitchen.

INGREDIENTS

FOR THE SALMON AND VEGETABLES
4 salmon fillets
1 courgette, cut into equal-sized batons
Half a butternut squash, sliced into equal-sized batons
Two large carrots, sliced into equal-sized batons
Wild chive flowers and radish, to garnish
Wild herb salad

FOR THE TERIYAKI SAUCE
125ml dark soy sauce
4 tbsp medium-dry sherry
2 tbsp rice vinegar or cider vinegar
2 tbsp runny honey

METHOD

● Start by making the teriyaki sauce. Mix the soy sauce and cornflour until you form a smooth paste. There should be no lumps or excess flour. Then stir in the remaining ingredients and mix thoroughly. Taste and adjust, to suit your palate. Set aside.

● Now prepare your vegetables. Cook in a pan of boiling water. The carrot should take about eight minutes, the butternut squash about five and the courgette about two – though it will depend how thickly you cut your vegetables. Remove from the pan and plunge into ice water, to retain their colour.

● Rinse your salmon fillets beneath cold running water and pat dry. Put in a large, non-metallic dish. Pour three quarters of the sauce over the salmon and cover with cling film. Rest on a plate in your fridge for at least two hours, so that the flavour infuses.

● Preheat your pan to medium-hot. While it's warming, brush a little more teriyaki sauce over the top of the salmon. Now place onto the griddle for three minutes, then turn by 90 degrees and put back on the heat for a further two minutes. Turn the salmon over and griddle until cooked through.

● Refresh your vegetables by plunging them back into boiling water for about 90 seconds, to reheat.

● Plate up as shown in picture.

CRISPY COD WITH SWEET-AND-SOUR SAUCE AND CHERRY TOMATOES

fish

I love the vibrant colour of this dish. It's an explosion of vibrant red, orange, yellow and green. It really is a beautiful recipe. I like to serve it in a shallow bowl, so that the sticky sweet-and-sour sauce sits below the pieces of fruit and vegetable. Then I place the cod on top and I finish it with cherry tomatoes that are roasted in the oven, in a little balsamic vinegar. The flavours are stunning, and, like a number of my fish dishes, you should find it remarkably easy to make. Dishes like this give you the opportunity to make restaurant-standard food in the comfort of your own kitchen.

INGREDIENTS

4 cod fillets
Generous handful white breadcrumbs
100g each pineapple, cucumber and carrot, all diced
100g cherry tomatoes and four strands of cherry vine tomatoes as well, with around four tomatoes on each vine
1 red onion, diced
1 egg, beaten
1 tsp balsamic vinegar
Cooking oil
Sweet-and-sour sauce (see page 19)

METHOD

- Make the sweet-and-sour sauce.
- Coat the fish with the beaten egg and then dredge it through the breadcrumbs. Plunge into the deep fat fryer at around 180C. Fry until golden brown, which should take around five minutes. Monitor to make sure you do not overcook – you can check by inserting a cooking thermometer into the centre of the fish; make sure it has reached a core temperature of 75C.
- Stir-fry the vegetables and pineapple in a wok. The carrot will take the longest, followed by the pineapple and the cherry tomatoes. Add in the sweet-and-sour sauce.
- Separately, drizzle the vine tomatoes with balsamic vinegar and roast in a 180C oven for 10 minutes.
- Assemble as shown, and garnish with dill.

PRAWN, RED GURNARD AND NOODLE IN A COCONUT-AND-LEMONGRASS SAUCE

fish

There are so many things to love about this dish. It's stunning, visually, thanks to the golden sweet potato crisp that encircles the red gurnard and sits on top of the noodles and prawns. It adds colour and texture. I add clams to my dish, for extra flavour, and garnish with edible flowers (in this case I've used wild garlic flowers). The prawns add colour and texture and the noodles and creamy lemongrass sauce make it a richly satisfying bowl of food. This is a particular favourite of mine.

INGREDIENTS

20 king prawns
16 clams
4 red gurnard fillets, cut into thin strips
1 sweet potato
250g noodles
400ml coconut cream
Juice of 1 lime
1 kaffir lime leaf
1 stalk lemongrass
Pinch of sugar
1 tbsp fish sauce

METHOD

- Prepare the sauce first. Add the coconut cream to a heavy-bottomed saucepan and add in the kaffir lime leaf, lemongrass stalk, sugar, fish sauce and lime juice. Reduce slightly, then set aside.
- Using a fine grater, grate long, fine strands of sweet potato and then gently wrap them around the goujouns of red gurnard. When the fish is completely wrapped, deep fry the fish in oil at 180C, until golden brown.
- While the fish is frying, add the clams and prawns to the coconut sauce and simmer until cooked. Set aside.
- Finally, blanch the noodles in boiling water for two minutes until soft. Drain and divide between four dishes, followed by the prawns and the clams. Coat in sauce. Now stack the red gurnard goujons on the top. Garnish with a wild garlic flower.

MONKFISH AND PRAWN GREEN THAI CURRY WITH VEGETABLES AND FRAGRANT RICE

fish

I love the presentation of this dish. The pieces of monkfish sit on top of a timbale of rice, and large king prawns, with their beautiful pink-orange colour, tower above it all. It sits in a small moat of Thai green curry and is decorated with cubes of vegetables and vibrant pieces of chilli. It's a hearty, filling dish that is packed with complementary flavours. I like to decorate my prawns with crispy vermicelli noodles, to add a little pizzazz.

INGREDIENTS

4 × 250g monkfish tails, skinned and boned
12 large, fresh king prawns, deveined
Green curry paste (see page 21)
1 tbsp fish sauce
1 tbsp sugar
200ml coconut cream
50g bamboo shoots
50g aubergine
250g Thai jasmine rice
375ml water

METHOD

- Steam the rice for around 15 minutes, until tender and soft.
- Fry the Thai green curry paste in a hot pan. Then add the fish sauce, sugar and coconut cream. Add the vegetables and cook until tender – it should take about two or three minutes.
- Add the fish. The monkfish should cook through in four or five minutes, so that it is white through. The prawns will take a little less time. You will know that they are cooked when they turn pink. The curry will simmer as the fish cooks. Remove from the heat once cooked.
- To serve, place the rice in a timbale then plate up in a large-sized dinner bowl or round plate. Place the monkfish on top of the rice. Stack the prawns on top of the monkfish. Swoosh the green curry around the side of the rice and fish.

THAI FISH THREE WAYS, WITH WASABI SAUCE

fish

This is a delightfully light dish that features salmon, sea bass and mackerel. It combines sweet salty flavours with a delightful kick, which comes from the wasabi sauce. It looks stunning on the plate and the idea of have three separate components appeals to me greatly. I like the idea of my guests being able to graze.

The trick to this dish is to use the freshest fish possible. When you buy your fish, make sure its scales and eyes are glistening.

INGREDIENTS

For the fish
350g salmon fillet
350g sea bass fillet
350g mackerel fillet
Small packet dried seaweed, to coat the outside of the mackerel

For the marinade
150ml rice wine vinegar
1 tbsp sugar
2 large red chillies, deseeded
2 tbsp fish sauce
1 clove garlic
2 tsp light soy sauce
Dill to garnish

For the wasabi sauce
4 tbsp mayonnaise (preferably homemade)
1 tsp wasabi paste
1 tbsp double cream
1 tbsp cooking oil
4 slices brown bread

METHOD

- Bone the fish, or make sure your fishmonger has done so. Take each piece of fish and slice thinly – they should be no more than 5mm thick.
- Combining all marinade ingredients in a bowl. Put each of the three fish into separate bowls and cover each of them with the marinade, leaving for around 30 minutes. Do not leave the fish any longer, otherwise it will slowly start to 'cook'. The object is simply to give the fish flavour, not mask the taste of it.
- Now cook the mackerel. First, pat the dried seaweed against the flesh so as to coat the outside. Pour a little vegetable oil into a hot pan and cook through. Serve the mackerel in a small bread cone, made by wrapping a slice of bread around a rolling pin and cooking in an oven at 180C for five minutes. It will retain its shape when cooled.
- Make the wasabi sauce by putting the mayonnaise, wasabi paste and double cream into a bowl with the cooking oil. Combine until the paste is runny.
- To serve, use long plates. Lay the sea bass together in thin strips, so that they overlap, at one end of the plate. Roll the salmon strips together using cling film to form a rose shape. Dot the wasabi sauce alongside. Garnish with micro leaves or salad. Place the mackerel nests at the other end of the plate.

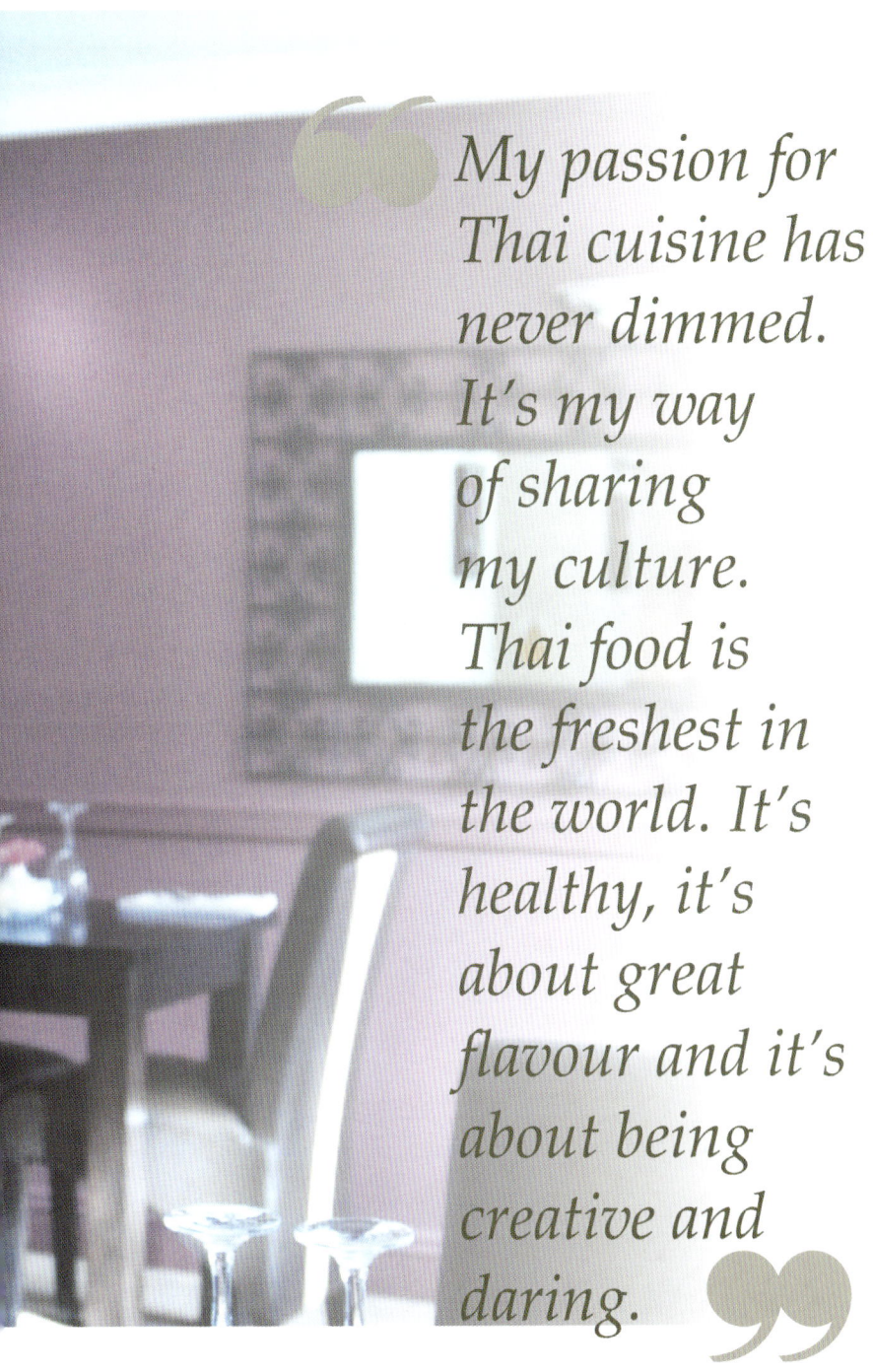

> My passion for Thai cuisine has never dimmed. It's my way of sharing my culture. Thai food is the freshest in the world. It's healthy, it's about great flavour and it's about being creative and daring.

Meat

THAI GREEN CURRY WITH CHICKEN

MEat

This is one of the classic Thai dishes and there are lots of different versions of it. The curry gets its name from its colour, which comes from the fresh green chillies used in the paste. It tends to be hotter than red curry – though you can turn the heat up or down by adjusting the volume of green chilli and coconut cream. The consistency of the dish can also be adjusted by using more or less coconut cream.

Thai green curry can be made using a variety of ingredients. You can add beef, pork, chicken or fish balls. Alternatively, you can make vegetarian versions, using vegetables of your choice. My top tip for anybody making a Thai green curry is to use the freshest ingredients possible. That's the way to bring out the best possible flavour.

INGREDIENTS

2 tbsp green curry paste
2 tbsp cooking oil
1 tbsp fish sauce
2 breasts of chicken, sliced into strips
Handful of Thai aubergines (optional)
400ml coconut cream
Pinch of sugar
125g bamboo shoots, sliced
For garnish – 1 large, thinly sliced red chilli, handful of Thai sweet basil, handful of fresh peppercorns

METHOD

- Heat the oil in a wok over a high heat and then add the green curry paste for a minute or two. The high heat will bring out all of the flavour.
- Add the chicken and cook.
- Now add half of the coconut cream. Continue to move vigorously around the pan, so that all of the pieces of chicken cook through.
- Add the vegetables and cook through (you want them to retain their texture, so don't overcook), then add the other half of the coconut cream and take off the heat. Add the fish sauce, to season.
- Garnish with chilli, basil leaves and peppercorns.
- Serve with rice.

THAI RED CURRY WITH CHICKEN, MANGO AND ASPARAGUS

Thai red curry is another classic dish. As with the green curry, there are a number of different varieties. Some are made with shrimp pastes, which means they cannot be served for vegetarians; others omit that ingredient. You can turn the heat up or down by adjusting the quantities of chilli and coconut cream.

You can also add lots of different ingredients to suit your palate. Chicken, beef, pork, duck, shrimp, tofu and fish balls are all popular. For this particular dish, I like to add asparagus and mango. If you add the mango and asparagus into the dish when you are making the curry, you'll give the dish even more flavour – the sweetness of the mango and the fresh grassiness of the asparagus. If you are focused on presentation, you can scorch the mango first on a hot griddle, which helps to caramelise the outside.

INGREDIENTS
2 tbsp red curry paste
2 tbsp cooking oil
1 tbsp fish sauce
2 breasts of chicken, sliced into strips
Half a ripe mango
Asparagus shoots – 8 stems
400ml coconut cream
Pinch of sugar
125g bamboo shoots, sliced
For garnish: sliced red chilli and Thai sweet basil

METHOD
- Put the cooking oil into a hot wok and add the curry paste. Stir fry for a minute or two.
- Add the chicken and sear, then add half of the coconut cream. Continue to stir vigorously, so that the chicken cooks through.
- Now add all of the vegetables. Continue to stir-fry.
- Add the fish sauce and sugar. Check the seasoning and adjust, to suit. Then add the other half of the coconut cream. Take off the heat.
- Garnish with chilli and basil.
- Serve with rice.

MASSAMAN CURRY WITH BEEF

The recipe for massaman curry is centuries old and it is most commonly made with beef, though it can be made with pork, chicken, tofu, duck or vegetables. It is a universally popular dish – in 2011 it was voted top in a CNN poll to find the world's 50 most delicious dishes.

One of the delights of this dish – and of all Thai cuisine – is that you can let your imagination run riot and incorporate a wide variety of ingredients. I like to combine the strong robust flavours of root vegetables. Adding a roast potato, purple potato, red onion and sweet potato all adds huge flavour. The addition of a cinnamon stick also gives the dish a delicious warmth, as well as striking visual contrast. You can garnish to your heart's content, using small slices of red chilli, or spring onion. Crushed peanuts or tiny fried slices of onion also add a further flourish. By incorporating layers of flavour and adding height to your dish, your guests can't fail to be impressed. We eat with all of our senses, including our sight – so with this dish your guests will be dazzled by the flavours, the textures and the colours. You can elevate this dish from the simple to the sensational.

INGREDIENTS

2 tbsp massaman curry paste
2 tbsp cooking oil
500g diced stewing beef
400ml coconut cream
100ml water
Cinnamon stick
Cardamom pods (1 tsp, or 10 pods)
5 shallots, peeled and whole
2 tbsp palm sugar
1 tsp sea salt
1 tbsp tamarind paste
1 handful crushed roasted peanuts
Vegetables – 1 potato, half a sweet potato, 2 parsnips, 1 purple potato (optional)

METHOD

- Halve all of the vegetables and roast until cooked and tender. That will depend to a certain extent on the size of the vegetables, but it should take about 25 minutes at 180C. Make sure all of the vegetable pieces are the same size, so that they cook evenly. Once cooked, set aside.
- Add the oil to a hot wok and sear the beef.
- Add half of the coconut cream, then the water. Turn down the heat and simmer very slowly over a gentle heat until the beef is tender. Add in the cinnamon stick while you are simmering, so that the flavours infuse.
- When the beef is cooked, add the remaining ingredients into the pan and turn up the heat. Then add in the remaining half of the coconut cream.
- Garnish and serve.

CHEF'S TIP: This is a great dish for the slow cooker. If you're going out to work, you can simply put all of the ingredients into the slow cooker and leave it for the whole day. When you get home, you'll have meltingly tender beef and a wonderfully fragrant curry.

DUCK WITH ORANGE SAUCE

Meat

Duck with orange is a dish that is loved around the world. It is cooked in so many different ways: the French love *Canard à l'orange*, the Americans have their own super-sized version, and the Chinese enjoy a version that is served with crispy duck.

This dish is one of my favourites because it includes so many different flavours. There is sweetness from the sugar and the orange; sharp, zesty acid from the orange peel; and heat from the cracked black pepper. You can adjust the dish to suit your own palate: if you like it hotter, add in more pepper, if you like it more sour, add in more zest; if you like it sweeter, add in more sugar or orange juice. One of the secrets of success is in using freshly squeezed orange juice. For the best results, buy extra oranges and squeeze your own.

INGREDIENTS

2 duck breasts
2 tbsp oil
2 oranges
1 tbsp demerara sugar
1 tsp cracked black pepper
1 tsp sea salt
1 red pepper, diced
1 yellow pepper, diced
150ml freshly squeezed orange juice
Orange zest and basil leaves to garnish

METHOD

- Score the duck breasts and set aside. Add half of the oil to a hot wok and then add the duck. Place it skin-side down, so that you scorch the skin and render out some of the fat. Once it is cooked through, rest. You can cook the duck in the oven, if you prefer. Again, score the skin first, then place it skin-side down in hot oil in the wok, before removing and cooking through in a 180C oven. Check with your guests how they like it to be cooked; most people will like it pink.
- Peel the oranges and cut into thick slices. Griddle for a minute on either side, so that there are light scorch marks. This helps with the caramelisation process, which gives the orange a deep, rich flavour.
- Make the sauce by adding orange juice, sugar, pepper and sea salt to a pan, then reducing by half. It will go quite sticky. If you want a more intense flavour and a stickier texture, just continue to reduce.
- Add the orange slices to the plate and slice the duck, rolling into flowers and placing on top. Garnish with the chopped pepper basil leaves and orange zest and then pour over the orange sauce.

Meat

I love cooking with fruit from south-east Asia and lychees are great to add to a dish. They have a delicate white pulp and a floral, sweet flavour. If you're trying to cook this dish, seek out fresh lychees – when lychees are canned, they lose a lot of their perfume-like flavour, so make sure you use fresh ones from a Chinese supermarket.

Lychees are popular throughout south-east Asia, particularly in China, Malaysia, Vietnam and Thailand. They have a great history; they were being used more than 2000 years BC.

The method for this dish is very similar to that for duck with orange sauce.

INGREDIENTS

2 duck breasts
2 tbsp red curry paste
2 tbsp oil
1 large handful of lychees (use canned only if that is all you can find)
400ml coconut cream
100g cherry tomatoes
1 tsp palm sugar
1 tbsp fish sauce
Sweet Thai basil to garnish

METHOD

- Score the duck breasts and set aside. Now add half of the oil to a hot wok and then add the duck. Place it skin-side down, so that you scorch the skin and render out some of the fat. Once it is cooked through, rest. You can cook the duck in the oven, if you prefer. Again, score the skin first, then place it skin-side down in hot oil in the wok, before removing and cooking through in a 180C oven. Check with your guests how they like it to be cooked; most people will like it pink. Rest the duck, once cooked.
- Add the remainder of the oil to the wok and cook the paste with coconut cream. Add the sugar, fish sauce, lychees and cherry tomatoes.
- Put the duck into the sauce and continue to cook until the sauce is bubbling.
- Remove from the heat, garnish and serve with rice.

LAMB CUTLETS IN SWEET CHILLI SAUCE

Meat

Meat has many different uses in Thai cooking. I live in Shropshire, a beautiful part of the UK that borders Wales. The farmland in Shropshire is rich and there is plenty of exceptional pasture. The region produces great meat, including lamb, and so I like to find new ways of incorporating local ingredients into my dishes. This is one example. The robust, savoury flavour of lamb works brilliantly with the mild heat and sweetness of my sweet chilli sauce. So I like to combine those different flavours.

I use local ingredients where possible: I have a number of beef dishes, for example, that use produce from our great local farmers. When you attempt this dish, buy your meat from a local butcher and ask them about its provenance. You'll find the quality of the meat is usually higher than that from a supermarket because it will often be locally sourced and hung for longer, so that the flavours develop.

INGREDIENTS

8 cutlets
1 tbsp oyster sauce to marinate the lamb
1 handful chopped mixed herbs – for this dish, use mint, thyme, parsley and coriander
Baby leaf salad
Sweet chilli sauce (see page 17)
1 tbsp cooking oil

METHOD

- This is a simple dish to cook. First, marinate the lamb in the oyster sauce so that the flavours infuse. The longer you can leave the lamb the better – an hour or two is great – but don't worry if you're pushed for time.
- Now griddle the cutlets until they are cooked through. Rest the meat, once cooked.
- Mix the salad leaves and the herbs together. Arrange those leaves on the plate and then place the cutlets on top. Dress with the sweet chilli sauce and serve.

BEEF WITH MUSHROOM IN OYSTER SAUCE

Meat

This is another dish that was inspired by the great quality of produce that's on my doorstep. As a restaurateur I have great relationships with my suppliers – including my butcher. He'll often come to the restaurant to tell me what he has in stock.

I have developed this particular dish over time, because the beef that he supplies is so fantastic. I tend to use fillet steak for this dish, though you can use rump if you prefer. Don't be afraid to adjust the dish to suit your palate. For instance, you might decide to use a greater selection of mushrooms, or add different garnishes. As with other dishes, you can turn the heat up or down to suit by simply adding more pepper and garlic. If you want a more savoury and intense flavour, add a little more oyster sauce.

INGREDIENTS

250g fillet beef, sliced
4 tbsp oyster sauce
1 tsp cracked black pepper
1 sliced red onion
Half a red pepper, half a yellow pepper and half a green pepper, each finely diced
250g mushrooms – I like to use a 50:50 mix of oyster and chestnut, though you can adapt to suit
1 tbsp cooking oil
1 clove garlic
Pinch of sugar
Sliced spring onion to garnish

METHOD

- Add the cooking oil to the pan and heat. Now add the garlic and onion and cook through. You want to get a nice caramelisation, so that their flavours stand up to the delicious beef.
- Add the beef and the mushrooms – your pan should be really hot. Cook both through, then add the oyster sauce – it will sizzle when it hits the pan.
- Add the diced pepper and continue to cook – you want to heat it through without letting it become soggy.
- Add the cracked black pepper and the pinch of sugar, and adjust the seasoning. Garnish and serve.

CHICKEN WITH CHILLI AND GINGER

Meat

This dish is a real classic. It combines many of the elements that make for great Thai cooking: there's a balance of heat and sweetness. Be careful when you make it that you get the right combination of ingredients – too much ginger will drown out the other flavours, so have a care.

This is a simple, rustic dish that doesn't take long to cook. It's a classic example of why Thai food is so much fun. You can arrive home from work, put all of these ingredients into a hot wok and within minutes you've got a delicious, flavoursome dish.

INGREDIENTS

2 chicken breasts, thinly sliced
2 stems ginger, thinly sliced
2 tbsp cooking oil
50ml chicken stock
1 tbsp fish sauce
1 tsp sugar
500g beansprouts
1 spring onion, sliced
1 large red chilli, sliced
1 red pepper and 1 yellow pepper, both thinly sliced
A scattering of mint leaves
1 red onion, finely sliced
1 clove of garlic, crushed

METHOD

- Heat the oil in the pan and add the garlic and onion. Caramelise.
- Add the chicken and cook through.
- Add all the vegetables when the chicken is just about cooked. You don't want to cook the vegetables for too long, otherwise they will become soggy. You want to cook them so they are just heated through and retain their texture.
- Now add the chicken stock and the sugar. Check the seasoning. If you're happy with the taste, you might not need to use the fish sauce – it's in the list of ingredients to add saltiness, but if you've used a salty stock you might not need to use it. You're looking for a balance of sweet, salty heat.
- Serve.

MINCED PORK WITH CHILLI AND BASIL

Meat

This is one of my absolute favourites because it's so simple. As with other dishes, the secret is in using the best-quality ingredients. Seek out good-quality meat and make sure you track down sweet Thai basil. The beauty of sweet Thai basil is that it retains its flavour under higher cooking temperatures than other varieties of the herb. If you track down a good supplier, you'll be able to find different types of basil, including holy basil and lemon basil. Remember the golden rule: the fresher the ingredients, the better the taste.

INGREDIENTS

500g minced pork
2 tbsp cooking oil
3 cloves garlic, crushed
1 tbsp fish sauce
1 large red chilli, sliced – if you want a spicy dish, put in more
1 spring onion, sliced
Handful of sweet Thai basil

METHOD

- It couldn't be simpler. Add the oil to a hot wok and stir fry the pork until cooked.
- Add the garlic, chilli and spring onion. Cook through, while retaining the texture of the chilli and spring onion.
- Take off the heat, garnish with sweet Thai basil and serve.

STIR-FRY PORK WITH GREEN VEGETABLES

Meat

This is a mix-and-match favourite. I'm a huge fan of this recipe, but you can use different ingredients if you like. If you prefer chicken, use that. If you prefer beef, use that. Similarly, if you prefer different types of greens, use them. I've added in asparagus, though that's optional. You really only want to use that when it's in season – imported varieties do not have anywhere near as much flavour as English asparagus in season.

It's a mild dish and you're looking to let the vegetables stand out – in many ways, they are the star of this dish.

INGREDIENTS
1 pork fillet, approximately 500g, sliced
1 tbsp cooking oil
4 pak choi
A good handful of broccoli stems
4 spring onions
8 stems asparagus (optional)
1 tsp sesame seeds
1 tbsp oyster sauce
Pinch of sugar
2 garlic cloves, crushed
1 red chilli for garnish

METHOD
- The method for this dish is as simple as the method for minced pork with chilli and sweet Thai basil. Simply add the oil to a hot wok and then add the pork and garlic. Stir-fry, until cooked through.
- Add in the vegetables, then the oyster sauce, sugar and sesame seeds.
- Add a pinch of sugar at the end and adjust the seasoning, to taste. Serve.

AUBERGINE AND CHINESE SAUSAGE FRIED RICE

Rice, Noodles, Vegetables

When I began to cook, as a young child, we made do with the things that we had grown or bought at market. Growing up in Thailand, we didn't have access to vast supermarkets or specialist delis that could provide ingredients from around the world. We had vegetables and fish, rice and herbs; that was pretty much it.

The thing I learned from those days was to be creative. You can conjure all sorts of magical dishes from a few humble ingredients if you use your imagination. The sort of humble, peasant food that I grew up on can be transformed into exciting, visually stunning restaurant-class dishes: all you need is imagination. This is a perfect example.

INGREDIENTS

1 aubergine
300g cooked rice
50g raisins or sultanas
1 tsp cinnamon powder
2 tbsp cooking oil
1 tbsp mixed peppers, diced
2 sweet Chinese sausages, thinly sliced
1 tbsp fish sauce
½ tbsp sugar
Juice of ½ a lemon
1 egg
Coriander oil (chopped fresh coriander mixed with extra virgin olive oil)

METHOD

● Slice the aubergine thinly and griddle both sides with a tiny bit of oil, but not much. You want to cook through until charred on the outside and softened within. Put to one side
● Add oil into a searing hot pan, then scramble the egg. Add the raisin, peppers, cinnamon and sausage, and fry off.
● Add the cooked rice, together with the fish sauce, sugar and lemon juice.
Assemble in timbale rings, with slices of aubergine, followed by rice, then further aubergine and so on. Press the layers down so that when you remove the ring the tower does not collapse.
● Use slices of the griddled aubergine to make a rose on the top. Dress with coriander oil and additional pepper dice.

CHEF'S TIP: If possible, make sure you buy Chinese sausage for this recipe. It has a hint of sweetness, which makes it perfect for the dish. You will find supplies online and in most Chinese supermarkets or grocers.

Cook your rice by steaming for 20 minutes, until soft.

BEEF WITH UDON NOODLE AND SESAME SEED

rice, Noodles, Vegetables

Udon noodles are delicious. They are normally associated with Japanese cuisine, but I like to use them in Thai recipes because they are filling and nutritious. They carry the flavours of a dish really well.

The flavours of the sauce in which the beef is stir-fried coat the exterior of the noodle so that every mouthful is lick-smackingly, mouthwateringly delicious. Chefs use rolling pins as long as their leg when they are making fresh udon. However, you do not have to go to those lengths. You will be able to buy udon at most Chinese supermarkets or grocery stores. They are also available online.

INGREDIENTS
300g beef fillet, cut into thin strips
1 clove garlic
2 tbsp cooking oil
250g udon noodles
2 tsp sesame seeds, pan-roasted
2 tbsp oyster sauce
1 tsp sugar
1 red pepper, cut into thin strips
Salad leaves to dress

METHOD
- Cook the udon noodles in boiling water for three minutes until soft. Drain and leave to stand for a moment.
- In a searingly hot pan, add the cooking oil and fry off the garlic. Add the strips of beef, then the strips of pepper. Now add the udon, oyster sauce and sugar and stir vigorously, so that the flavours combine.
- Garnish a plate with salad leaves and serve on those. Sprinkle with the sesame seeds.

CHEF'S TIP: I always use fillet for this dish because the texture of the beef is critical. There are dishes when it's okay to use more flavoursome cuts, such as rump. But for this dish, I like to make sure the beef is meltingly tender and that's why fillet is best.

CHICKEN SATAY WITH RICE NOODLE CAKE

Rice, Noodles, Vegetables

One of the wonders of Thai cooking is that you can mix and match so many different flavours. There is a store cupboard of staples, such as rice and noodles; a number of different fish and meat components that work well, from prawns to pork and from monkfish to chicken; and then there are a number of sauces and dips, from satay to sweet-and-sour, and from red curry to green curry.

This dish takes a mix-and-match approach and brings together different textures and tastes. Rather than serving noodles in a conventional way, I like to make these into a cake, by pressing them together once they are cooked. That means you can cut them into different shapes and present them as you wish: flat on a plate or in a small tower, with the satay sauce poured over the top.

The satay chicken with satay sauce works brilliantly with the noodles. It's a fun dish.

INGREDIENTS

1 quantity of chicken satay (see page 42)
1 quantity of satay sauce (see page 16)
600g of medium egg noodles
1 tbsp crushed roasted peanuts
1 handful coriander leaf, for garnish
1 sliced red chilli, for garnish

METHOD

- Cook your noodles in boiling water for three minutes and then drain. Rest for a few minutes.
- Now put the noodles into a square tin or similar vessel, then press down with a heavy weight. If possible, leave for around an hour, so that the noodles cool and stick together. When you remove the weight, the starch in the noodles will have acted like glue and they will have formed a cake.
- Lay the noodle cake flat on a board. Cut oblong shapes, and then cut the oblongs in half, diagonally, so that you have elongated wedges.
- To serve, take the wedges of noodle cake and lay two together. Now layer two chicken satay strips on top. Add two more pieces of noodle cake and then add two further satay strips. This dish is like jenga. You can play around with the shapes until you achieve what you'd like!
- Now drizzle a quantity of satay sauce over the tower and garnish with red chilli and coriander.

101

EGG FRIED RICE

rice, Noodles, Vegetables

Most chefs from South East Asia have their own recipe for fried rice. I've included three in this book, though there are literally thousands of different variations. The basic recipe uses steamed rice that is then added to a wok and stir-fried with other ingredients, including egg. There really is no limit to the ingredients that you use.

It is vitally important to use pre-cooked rice that has been thoroughly drained. If there is too much moisture in the rice, you will find it becomes mushy and soggy.

In this instance, my recipes are intended merely as a guide. If you want to add additional flavour by adding onions, shallots, more garlic, or different types of vegetable and herbs, then go ahead.

INGREDIENTS
300g cooked rice
2 free-range eggs
2 tbsp cooking oil
1 clove garlic
Pinch of sugar
Pinch of salt

METHOD
- This really is the simplest of dishes. In a searingly hot pan, cook the garlic in the oil.
- Crack your eggs and scramble, so that they are cooked through.
- Stir in the rice and add the sugar and salt.
- You can garnish as you wish, with spring onion, wild garlic flowers, chive flowers or whatever is available. Taking care to make the effort with your presentation will transform the dish.

CHEF'S TIP: Where possible, use free-range eggs. They have better yolks than those from battery hens and the golden colour, coupled with the extra flavour, will make your dish stand out.

CHICKEN FRIED RICE

rice, Noodles, Vegetables

Chicken fried rice is perennially popular. You might choose to serve it as a quick supper, using left-over rice. It's a dish that can be made in five minutes flat – by the time you've cooked your chicken the dish will be complete. Feel free to add in whatever is in your store cupboard. So, for instance, if you have half a packet of cashew nuts, add them to the dish for extra bite and texture. If you have peppers or other vegetables, add those in too.

The dish is perfect as a simple supper but you can also use it as a side dish with other recipes. So, for instance, you might choose this to go with a chicken green curry, or to accompany a chicken satay. Dishes like chicken fried rice are cooked throughout Thailand, including at street markets. Often, vendors will cook the dish from scratch in a matter of minutes.

INGREDIENTS
One batch of egg fried rice (see page 102)
2 large tomatoes
2 tbsp peppers, diced
1 carrot, in thin strips
1 tbsp oil
225g chicken thighs, boned and cut roughly
Coriander leaves and salad leaves to garnish

METHOD
- This recipe uses chicken thighs, which have a bit more flavour than breast. You can use breast, thinly sliced, if you prefer. Add the oil to a searingly hot pan and cook your chicken.
- Add the carrot and peppers and cook until they begin to soften.
- Add in the egg fried rice and then the tomatoes, so that they take on a little heat. Be careful not to cook for too long – you don't want them to disintegrate. It should take a matter of minutes from start to finish.
- To serve, garnish with coriander leaves and salad leaves.

PRAWN FRIED RICE

rice, Noodles, Vegetables

I've never quite understood why so many people make a post-work dash to the takeaway when it is so simple to cook dishes like this. As with the other fried rice dishes, you can add in extra ingredients to suit your palate. You can also vary the seasonings, if you wish. So, for instance, you might want to add in a twist of lime and serve with a few lime wedges. Alternatively, you might want to add in two tablespoons of Thai curry paste, to give it a little kick. The possibilities are endless.

If you prefer a saltier dish, add in a tablespoon of fish sauce, plus a little extra to serve. If you want to add colour and texture, add in some shredded cucumber, sliced red chilli and a few extra coriander leaves. My recipe for prawn fried rice is intended as a starting point for you. That's the beauty of Thai cooking: it is adaptable and you can add in extra flavour to suit your own tastes.

INGREDIENTS

1 quantity of egg fried rice (see page 102)
1 tbsp oil
300g king prawns, peeled and deveined
175g green beans, sliced
2 large tomatoes
A handful of coriander leaves and salad leaves to garnish

METHOD

- Add the oil to a searingly hot pan and cook your prawns.
- Add the green beans and cook until they begin to soften. Add in the egg fried rice and then the tomatoes, so that they take on a little heat. Be careful not to cook for too long, you don't want them to disintegrate. It should take a matter of minutes from start to finish.
- To serve, garnish with coriander leaves and salad leaves.

KING PRAWNS WITH EGG NOODLE, BEETROOT NOODLE AND SWEET-AND-SOUR SAUCE

rice, Noodles, Vegetables

I got the idea for this dish from a dinner that I ate at La Bécasse, in Ludlow. The chef, Will Holland, who was kind enough to write the foreword for *Cook Thai*, had created incredible textures and shapes using vegetables. Will is a genius, in my opinion. He is constantly innovating and creating new ways to present food. That keeps things fresh and interesting, both for the chefs in the kitchen and the customers.

I decided to make beetroot noodles for this dish using a turning slicer, which can be bought online or from most decent cook shops. They don't cost much and are worth their weight in gold. The combination of beetroot noodles with conventional noodles is visually stunning; it also offers a flavour contrast. Sweet-and-sour sauce works perfectly with this dish; it complements the sweetness of the beetroot and saltiness of the prawn.

INGREDIENTS

1 quantity of sweet-and-sour sauce (see page 19)
12 raw king prawns, deveined and cleaned. Make sure you leave the tail in the shell
600g of medium egg noodles (use fresh, not dried)
1 beetroot

METHOD

- First, prepare your beetroot noodles. Take a single beetroot and turn it on the turning slicer, so that you have an elongated 'noodle'. Set aside.
- Take half of the uncooked noodles and wrap them around the prawns. You have left the tail in the shell so that you can pick them up to eat them. The idea is to have a crispy, crunchy outer shell and a soft, warm prawn inside. Deep-fry the noodle-wrapped prawns at around 180C until golden brown. Drain.
- Now cook the other half of your noodles, along with the beetroot noodle. It should take around three minutes to cook them, in boiling water. Drain.
- To serve, assemble as pictured, with a bed of beetroot and egg noodles on the plate and crispy, crunchy prawns piled high on top. Dress the plate with sweet-and-sour sauce.

CHEF'S TIP: If you don't have the time (or the patience) to wrap the prawns in noodles, you could use wonton wrappers instead, thereby adding crisp crunchy texture to the dish.

PAD THAI

rice, Noodles, Vegetables

Pad Thai is one of the all-time classic South East Asian dishes. It is actually of Vietnamese origin, but it is popular in Thailand and China, and throughout the region.

The dish has a strong association with Thailand and was made famous by Luang Phibunsongkhram, Prime Minister during the late 1930s and 1940s. He renamed the dish as part of a campaign to reduce domestic rice consumption. The Thai economy had become too dependent on rice exports and the Prime Minister wanted Thais to eat more noodles. His idea proved popular and Pad Thai became one of Thailand's national dishes.

Pad Thai has iconic status and has featured in a number of films. It was in the Thai film *Jao saao Pad Thai*, that the leading lady said she would marry whoever ate her Pad Thai for 100 days in a row.

INGREDIENTS

3 eggs
2 tbsp crushed roasted peanut
300g rice noodles
1 tbsp oil
1 tbsp tamarind paste
2 tbsp sugar
1 tbsp fish sauce
2 tbsp chopped pickled radish, available from Chinese grocers and supermarkets
2 spring onions, shredded
50g bean sprouts
100g fresh tofu
Wild garlic flowers and chive flowers to garnish (optional)

METHOD

- Blanch the noodles in hot water for three minutes and then drain. Put to one side and rest.
- Cut the fresh tofu into 2cm cubes and deep-fry at 180C until golden brown. Set aside.
- Crack two eggs and scramble; you want to create an omelette. Take it out of the pan, roll it up tightly, and slice diagonally into strips.
- Take the third egg and add it to a searingly hot pan, which contains the oil. Scramble. Add the chopped radish, then the tofu. Stir-fry for a moment. Add the fish sauce, sugar, tamarind paste and mix together.
- Now add the cooked noodles, spring onions and bean sprouts. Check the flavours before serving. There should be a good balance between sweet, sour and salty. Adjust the seasoning to suit your palate, by adding in extra fish sauce, sugar and tamarind paste, as required.
- Serve with the strips of omelette, and decorated with sliced red chilli and edible chive flowers, wild garlic or anything else that is available, such as coriander.

PORK WITH CRISPY NOODLE NESTS

rice, Noodles, Vegetables

I love the versatility of Thai ingredients, and noodles are a case in point. They go from one end of the texture spectrum to the other. They can be served soft or crispy, whichever you prefer.

This particular dish features crispy fried noodle nests, which add in a wonderful crunch. I like to add additional garnish by sprinkling the nest with diced peppers. The colours add a wonderful vibrancy to the dish, making it fresh and tasty.

INGREDIENTS

300g pork fillet, finely sliced
300g fresh egg noodles
1 spring cabbage, or spring greens
1 tbsp oil
1 carrot, cut into fine strips
1 clove garlic
1 tbsp peppers, diced
2 tbsp light soy sauce
Pinch of sugar

CHEF'S TIP: As with the beef dish with udon noodles and sesame seed (see page 98), it is essential that you use fillet for this dish. Shoulder and leg have more flavour but for this dish you are looking for a meltingly tender texture.

METHOD

● Start by making your noodle nest. Deep-fry the noodles by plunging into oil at around 180C. While the noodles are frying, stir them so that they clump together in a ball (make sure you don't burn your fingers while doing this). Use a knife or fork or similar implement and whisk them around, so that they aggregate.

● Once the noodles are cooked and turn golden brown, remove the nest from the oil and drain. Once they are cool enough to touch, use your hands to clump them together, if they are still a little pliable. They will set crisply as they dry and cool.

● Add the oil to a pan and stir-fry the pork. Add in the vegetables, and then the light soy sauce and sugar.

● Plate as shown, with the meat and vegetables on the bottom and the crispy noodle on top. Decorate with pepper and coriander.

SUSHI WITH DICED PEPPER AND PICKLED GINGER

rice, Noodles, Vegetables

Sushi has become one of the most popular dishes in the world and there are numerous variations. Served using fish, rice and vegetables, and accompanied by pickled ginger and wasabi, or soy sauce, there are numerous permutations.

This recipe is a simple version that gives you a beginner's guide to sushi. The best approach is to master this one first, then start adding more ingredients. Eventually, you'll find yourself becoming as creative as you wish; who knows, you may end up becoming a sushi master!

INGREDIENTS

200g sushi rice
1 tbsp peppers, different colours, diced (if you were to use other vegetables, such as carrot or cucumber, cut them into fine batons; they should all be of equal width and length)
1 packet seaweed wraps
2 tbsp rice wine vinegar
2 tbsp light soy sauce
Squeeze of lemon juice
Diced cucumber, red chilli and coriander
1 tsp pickled ginger

METHOD

● Rinse the rice until the water no longer runs cloudy.
● Cook your rice so that it is light, fluffy and sticky (an electric rice cooker is ideal for this). Season the rice with rice wine vinegar. If you want to add more flavour, you can add a little sugar and salt into the rice wine vinegar and stir it until it dissolves.
● Place your seaweed wraps onto a bamboo mat and cover with rice. Now place your vegetables in the centre of the rice. Finally, roll the bamboo mat around the seaweed sheets so that you get a long tube of seaweed wrapped rice, filled with vegetables.
● Once you've formed a long 'sausage' shape, simply cut into 3cm rolls which can be picked up with chopsticks. I serve this particular pepper sushi with pickled ginger and a light soy dip, which is made by combining the soy sauce, lemon juice and a little diced cucumber, red chilli and coriander.

desserts

I love desserts. As passionate as I am about the natural flavours of authentic Thai cuisine, I also have a secret passion for all things sweet. It's not just the taste that I enjoy, it's also the presentation. At weekends and on bank holidays, when the rest of the world is enjoying itself, you'll find me in my kitchen experimenting. I'll happily spend months perfecting my macaroons, or I'll spend an age creating intricate and imaginative new sugar shards, or chocolate nests. We all love a good pud – and I love mine to be the prettiest of all. When you're creating a pudding, concentrate not just on the flavour, but on the presentation too. Make every dish a work of art. We use all of our senses when we're eating – so make your desserts as dramatic and exciting as a fireworks display.

desserts

INGREDIENTS

FOR PINEAPPLE CRISPS
1 ripe pineapple
Stock syrup – made from 100g sugar and 100ml water

FOR TART TATIN
1 whole pineapple
350g puff pastry (1 block of shop-bought is fine)
200g caster sugar
50g butter, cut into cubes

METHOD

● First make the crisps. Bring the stock syrup to the boil for about 10 minutes and reduce slightly. It should not go too thick or too sticky. Set aside.

● Now peel the ripe pineapple, removing all skin and husk, then thinly slice on a mandoline.

● Dip slices of pineapple into the stock syrup. Place the slices on a non-stick mat and put on a baking tray. Cook in a very low oven, at 100C, until the pineapple slices are dried out – the best method is to leave overnight and check in the morning. It could take as long as 24 hours. Cool on a wire rack, then store in an airtight container.

● Now make the tart. Peel the pineapple then cut into slices approximately 1.5cm thick. Remove the stem from the centre. In a pan, add the caster sugar over a low heat so that it forms a golden-coloured syrup, then add the butter.

● Add the pineapple and gently simmer on one side for 10 minutes. Turn over and cook on the other side for 10 minutes, or until golden brown. Leave to cool in the pan.

● Roll out your pastry and lay over the top of the pan. Now tuck the sides in, so that the pastry covers the cooked pineapple.

● Bake in a preheated oven at 180C until the pastry puffs up and is a golden colour – around 20 minutes.

● Remove the tart from the oven and leave to cool, then turn upside down onto a plate. Serve with a coconut sorbet or ice-cream (see page 125).

COCONUT PANNA COTTA WITH EXOTIC FRUITS

desserts

This is a delicious recipe and is one of the most eye-catching you'll find.

I like to make a tray of panna cotta, which I then cut into the required shape. You can make it into different shapes, if you wish, by pouring the panna cotta into different-shaped moulds. I decorate my panna cotta with a mixture of fruits and coulis – raspberry and apple work particularly well. Just cut out small pieces of sweet, juicy, vibrantly coloured flesh and decorate. I also like to add a few swishes of fruit coulis to the plate. There are plenty of variations for this recipe. You can add in different flavours, if you wish.

INGREDIENTS

570ml coconut cream
4 leaves of gelatine (platinum grade)
150g caster sugar

You will need moulds in which to set the panna cotta

METHOD

- Line your moulds with cling film. Make sure it lines all of the tin and hangs over the side, so that you can pull it out of the moulds with ease. Set aside.
- Soak the gelatine leaves in cold water, until soft. It should take around 10 minutes.
- Bring the coconut cream and sugar to the boil then take off the heat. Set aside.
- Squeeze any excess water from the gelatine and then stir it into the warm coconut cream so that the gelatine dissolves. Leave to cool.
- Pour the mixture into the moulds and leave it to set in the fridge for two to three hours. Once set, remove from the moulds and serve. Add mixed berries and fruit, or decorate with ornate sugar work.

THAI STICKY BLACK RICE PUDDING WITH MANGO ROSE

desserts

This is a particularly dramatic dessert. It can be served with fresh fruit, such as mango, and decorated with chocolate and fruit coulis. The colour of the black rice provides a stunning contrast to the other ingredients on the plate. It has wonderful flavour and delicious texture. The pinch of salt is the secret ingredient and it provides a great contrast to the sugar, giving it that unique Thai combination of sweet-salty. It's a winning dessert.

INGREDIENTS

250g Thai sticky black rice
150ml coconut cream
50g caster sugar
Pinch of salt
1 mango

METHOD

● Soak the rice in cold water for at least an hour, until it begins to soften, then rinse and steam the rice for 25 minutes, until gently cooked. It should be a little al dente – you don't want a mushy texture. Cook it in a rice cooker, if you prefer.

● When the rice is cooked put it into a pan and add the coconut cream, caster sugar and a pinch of salt. Heat through, until the rice absorbs the other ingredients and becomes sticky.

● I like to serve quenelles of rice with swirls of melted chocolate, fruit coulis, tuilles and a mango rose. Adding so much ornamentation to the plate transforms the dish.

For the mango rose

Take one mango and skin it. Now cut the mango into two halves following the flat sides of the seed. To each half, on a slant, cut 3mm thin slices, starting with the smaller slices and gradually progressing to the larger slices. Now bend each slice into a U-shape and arrange in overlapping circles starting from the centre.

BANANA FRITTER WITH COCONUT ICE-CREAM

desserts

One of the things that I love so much about this dessert is that it takes humble ingredients and elevates them into something very special. A little imagination, a little craft and a little time spent presenting the dessert elevates it from the ordinary into the extraordinary. I like to serve my banana fritters with coconut ice-cream. There's a wonderful contrast between the crunch of the banana fritter and the soft, silky ice-cream, which melts through the hot fritters when they are stacked high on the plate.

INGREDIENTS

For banana fritters
4 bananas
200g dessicated coconut
200ml sparkling water
85g plain flour
50ml honey
Cooking oil for frying

For coconut ice-cream
500ml coconut milk
150ml double cream
2 eggs
4 egg yolks
200g caster sugar

METHOD

● First, make the batter by combining the flour and sparkling water. Whisk until it is completely smooth and has a good consistency.

● Cut the bananas into batons – or be creative about the shapes that you want to use. Coat them in the batter and then dredge through the dessicated coconut, so that they are completed coated.

● Heat the oil until smoking hot. Then deep-fry the bananas until the batter is crisp and the coconut is a golden-brown colour. When cooked, remove the bananas and drain on kitchen paper, to remove any excess fat.

● To serve, stack into a tower and add a scoop of coconut ice-cream or sorbet (see below). You can also garnish with fresh fruit.

Ice-cream

● Put the coconut cream and double cream into a saucepan and simmer for two to three minutes, until it starts to foam. Take off the heat.

● Combine the eggs and egg yolks with the sugar. Blend together until you have a creamy consistency. Now pour the warm cream over the egg mixture and combine. Make sure the milk is not boiling, otherwise it will scramble the egg mixture. Stir quickly. Then place the bowl over a larger bowl of simmering water and continue to stir until it begins to thicken. Then cool and churn in an ice-cream maker.

Coconut sorbet

● Use the same method as for the ice-cream, but *omit the egg yolks and double cream*. Simply add the other ingredients into a blender and whisk. The blender will add air into the mix: make sure you use a fast speed. The mixture should be light and frothy. Now cool churn in an ice-cream maker.

EXOTIC FRUIT TOWER

126 COOK THAI WITH SUREE COATES

desserts

This is just a simple recipe to follow and yet it looks absolutely amazing. The secret is to make great coconut tuiles. After that, all you need is a great selection of fruit pieces and plenty of patience, so that your tower is stacked high and doesn't topple.

I like to serve this with mango sorbet and a white chocolate curl, as well as a sprinkle of desiccated coconut and a mint leaf. The key is to be imaginative. You don't have to use melon, if you prefer a different fruit. Use whatever is in season, whatever is at its best – and take your time – you don't want your tower to fall!

INGREDIENTS
Fresh fruit of choice
450ml stock syrup

FOR COCONUT TUILES
100g dessiccated coconut
2 egg whites
85g plain flour
100g icing sugar

FOR THE MANGO SORBET
350ml mango coulis, or two very ripe mangoes
350ml stock syrup
50g glucose syrup
Juice of 1 lime

METHOD
● First make the tuiles. Mix all the ingredients together in a food processor until you have a smooth paste. There should be no lumps.
● Make yourself a stencil by cutting a circle shape into the top of a margarine tub, or other plastic container. Now place the stencil on a non-stick mat on a baking tray. Spoon out enough mix to lightly cover the hole in the stencil – it should be very fine, just 1–2mm.
● Bake in a preheated oven at 160C for 10 minutes, or until golden. Leave to cool on a wire rack.
● Prepare the fruit – I have used a mango, a papaya, a melon and four passion fruits. Scoop out the mango, papaya and melon (not the passion fruit) with a Parisienne scoop. Scoop out as many balls as you can. Now heat the stock syrup until warm and gently warm the fruit. You do not want to overcook, otherwise it will become mushy. It should retain its firm texture.
● Make the mango sorbet. Blitz all of the ingredients together. Now transfer to a pan and slowly simmer for around 15 minutes. Pass through a sieve, so that the texture is completely smooth. Leave to cool.
Place into an ice-cream machine and churn until set. Freeze until required.

TO SERVE
Place small fresh-fruit pieces on the bottom of the plate. They should all be of an equal height. Now place a coconut tuile on top. Now arrange small balls of melon on top of the tuile. Place another tuile on top. Now add a third tuile and then garnish with further fruit. Add a final tuile and then add a scoop of mango sorbet and other decorative elements.

FRUIT FOOLS

desserts

I love fruit fools. They are light, creamy, colourful and deliciously tasty. You can use whatever fruit you like – I like to go for the freshest, most colourful and most tasty. I love lining up shot glasses that contain different flavours of fool (I call it a party on a plate!). There are myriad different recipes, which depend on how rich or light you want your fool to be. You can use mascarpone or crème fraîche, if you like. This recipe uses double cream.

INGREDIENTS
250ml double cream
50g icing sugar
Fruit purée

METHOD
- Add the icing sugar to the cream and then whisk to soft peaks.
- Purée three quarters of your fruit and retain the rest to use as garnish.
- Pipe the cream mixture into shot glasses, spooning fruit purée as you go. The idea is to have an equal amount of each, so there's an intoxicating blend of cream and fruit.
- I like to garnish the top of my fools with fruit, chocolate curls and mint. You can also decorate the plate by piping chocolate lines onto the surface and filling in any circles with dabs of fruit purée. The taste of these fools is a treat and they are the simplest dessert ever: it's just mix, pipe and dress. Make sure your presentation matches up to the amazing flavours and colours.

BLUEBERRY CHEESECAKE WITH WHITE CHOCOLATE SAUCE

desserts

This dessert is a real treat and, like the fruit fools, it's simple to make. Everybody loves a cheesecake, and this recipe is a doddle. Seasoning your mix with a dash of lemon juice will make all the difference. And when it comes to using your fruit, make sure that your blueberries are as fresh as can be. If you're in a different season, use whatever is in abundance – for instance cherries in spring, strawberries in summer and raspberries in autumn. You can also put together classic combinations, like peaches and strawberries or orange and pomegranate.

As with the fools, you can adapt the recipes to make the cheesecake lighter by using a mascarpone of crème fraîche. I'm a fan of the traditional method, however, which uses both full-fat cream cheese and double cream. This recipe gives you a really tangy cheesecake. If you want a creamier flavour, just change the proportions of cream and cream cheese to suit.

INGREDIENTS

For the cheesecake
300g full-fat cream cheese
100ml double cream, whisked to soft peaks
50g of caster sugar
Juice of ½ lemon
150g fresh blueberries, for garnish
150g digestive biscuits
75g melted butter

For white chocolate sauce
200g white chocolate
1 vanilla pod
100ml double cream, whisked to soft peaks

METHOD

● Mix the cream cheese and sugar together, then fold in the whisked double cream. Now season with the lemon juice. Set aside.

● For the biscuit base, crunch the digestives and set aside. Melt the butter on a medium heat (be careful that it does not burn) and incorporate the crushed biscuits into the butter. Press the mix into the base of a baking tin, or individual cylinders, and chill in the fridge until the mixture is cool and set.

● To finish, spoon the cream mixture onto the top of the biscuit base and then garnish with fresh fruit.

● For the sauce, simply melt the chocolate and then fold in the cream. Scrape the seeds from one vanilla pod and incorporate into the mix. Leave to cool in the fridge for an hour before using.

CHILLI CHOCOLATE TART WITH COCONUT SORBET AND CHOCOLATE-DIPPED CHILLI

desserts

This is a recipe that always gets people talking. Adding a chocolate-dipped chilli to the top of the dessert adds an element of fun. Not everyone will be brave enough to eat it, but it's always fun to find out who will and who won't. Use the best chocolate possible, such as Callebaut or Valrhona, and at least 72%, so that it's got lots of bittersweet flavour. In Shropshire, we have a great importer, Marou, which has won lots of awards for single-origin Vietnamese chocolate. You can taste the difference between each variety: some are mellow, others are bitter like coffee, some are fruity, some have elements of spice.

INGREDIENTS
FOR THE PASTRY
375g plain flour
300g soft butter
150g icing sugar
3 egg yolks
pinch of salt
zest of one lemon

FOR THE GANACHE
100ml double cream
1 large red chilli, split in half
125ml whole milk
3 egg yolks
150g dark chocolate
20g of soft butter
25g caster sugar

METHOD

● I tend to make my pastry in a food processor, so I use an all-in-one method. Add the ingredients to the blender and then mix until it becomes a smooth dough. There should be no flour or lumps, it should have an even, silky consistency. Now leave it in the fridge for a least an hour, wrapped in cling film, to rest.

● Take the pastry out of the fridge and roll it on a lightly dusted board until the pastry is approximately 2–3mm thick. You want the pastry to be light, thin and crisp. Be firm when you are rolling – you don't want to over-roll it. Assertive, strong rolls will get you there quickly.

● Line individual pastry cases, then leave for an hour in the fridge, covered in cling film.

● Now blind bake. Line the pastry cases with cling film – don't worry, it won't melt, the temperature in your oven won't go above 180C and cling film will tolerate that. Fill the pastry cases with rice, making sure it is well packed down, and cook at 180C for 20 minutes until golden brown. Remove from the oven, remove rice and cling film and leave on a wire rack to cool.

● Now make the ganache. Infuse the cream with the chilli by putting both in a heavy-bottomed pan over a medium heat and simmering gently for 10 minutes. Add the milk and continue to simmer. Then set aside.

● Cream together the egg yolks and the sugar, then set aside.

● Remove the chilli from the cream mixture, then add the mix to the eggs and sugar. Whisk vigorously. The cream mixture should not be boiling, otherwise the eggs will scramble.

● Add in the chocolate and make sure it combines. Add in the butter and combine. When cool, pipe into the pastry cases.

You can serve with a coconut ice-cream or coconut sorbet, along with chocolate curls.

LEMON POSSET WITH SHORTBREAD AND FRUIT

desserts

Lemon posset is delicious. It's also easy to make in your own kitchen. And, as with some of my other dessert recipes, you can transform it by spending time on your decorations and garnishes. I like to make sesame seed shortbreads to go with this, they have a delicious nutty taste and a delightful texture. You can also garnish with soft fruits; use whatever is sweet, in season and full of flavour.

INGREDIENTS

FOR THE LEMON POSSET
Juice of 5 lemons
300g caster sugar
500ml double cream

FOR THE SHORTBREAD
225g plain flour
150g soft unsalted butter
75g caster sugar
25g sesame seeds

METHOD

- Make the posset. Strain the lemon juice through a sieve and then place into a pan with the sugar. Now stir until dissolved, bringing to the boil. Remove from heat and set aside.
- In a separate pan, bring the cream to the boil. Now pour the boiled cream into the warm lemon/sugar mixture and pass through a sieve. Pour into serving dishes and place in the fridge to set.
- For the shortbread, cream the butter and sugar together, then add in the flour and sesame seeds. Mix well to form a dough. Cover with cling film and leave in the fridge to rest – an hour is great, but don't worry if you can only leave it for 10 minutes.
- Roll out the pastry to a thickness of 1cm. Cut into small biscuit-shaped pieces (I like oblongs about 1cm × 2.5cm, or small squares, 2.5cm × 2.5cm.
- Line a baking tray with baking parchment and place the shortbread shapes onto them. Put them back in the fridge for their second rest. Again, an hour's great, but don't worry if it's only 10 minutes. The purpose of the second rest is to chill the butter, to prevent the shortbreads from spreading when they go into the oven.
- Bake at 190C for about 15 minutes, or until golden brown. Cool on a wire rack.

petits fours

There's no better ending to the evening than coffee and petits fours. I love tiny nuggets of chocolate, melt-in-the-mouth macaroons, chocolate lollipops and deliciously crisp tuiles.

When you arrive at the end of a dinner, you want your guests to go out on a high. So though the end is in sight, remember to keep on pushing. Your guests will be thrilled that you've gone to so much time and trouble for them.

SHORTBREAD WITH ROSE PETALS

petits fours

These shortbread biscuits are decorated with delicate dried, crystallised rose petals, which add a light perfumed flavour and give your biscuits an air of luxury. It's worth spending a little extra time on then, to give your petits fours the 'wow factor'.

INGREDIENTS
225 plain flour
150g unsalted butter at room temperature
75g caster sugar

METHOD
- Cream the sugar and the butter, then add in the flour and blend until you form a smooth soft dough. Cover with cling film and leave to cool in the fridge for 10 minutes.
- Roll out the dough to a 1cm thickness. Cut into the relevant shape and then rest for a second time, to stop the biscuits from spreading out when they tray is in the oven.
- Cook at 180C for 15 minutes until golden brown. Decorate with chocolate and dried rose petals. Delish!

HONEYCOMB

Giant golden rocks of honeycomb add an impressive flourish to any dessert platter. The trick is in reheating the mixture after you've added your bicarbonate of soda.

INGREDIENTS
3 tsp bicarbonate of soda
4 tbsp golden syrup
200g granulated sugar

METHOD
- Melt the syrup and the sugar together, in a heavy-bottomed saucepan.
Heat to 150C (use a thermometer) then whisk in the bicarbonate. It will froth and foam. Now reheat for a further minute to reactivate the bicarbonate of soda, which helps to add in further air.
- Leave to set for two hours and then it should be brittle. Break into large chunks.

TUILES

petits fours

Tuiles are the moorish, thin and crispy shards of deliciousness that are added as garnishes to a variety of desserts, from panna cotta to exotic fruit towers. You can make them into any shape you like, by drawing a stencil on a plastic margarine tub, cutting that out, and then spreading mixture onto a heatproof mat. If you want circles, use a cup to make your stencil, if you want long spikes, use a ruler. You can achieve curved shapes by draping tuiles over curved surfaces, such as wine bottles or rolling pins.

Tuiles must be curved while still warm to prevent them from snapping. You can also add sesame seeds, drops of fruit coulis and other ornamentations.

INGREDIENTS
MAKES 30–40, DEPENDING ON SHAPE AND SIZE

2 egg whites
100g melted butter
100g icing sugar
100g plain flour

METHOD

- Mix all ingredients together to form a smooth paste and rest it in the fridge for at least two hours. If you use the mixture too soon, it will spread in the oven and lose its shape.
- Make your stencil: get a plastic lid and cut through so that you have a circle, spike or similar shape. Then spread a 2mm-thick layer through the stencil onto a non-stick mat on a baking tray. Leave a 2cm space between tuiles, so that they don't merge.
- Bake for 10 minutes at 170C until golden brown.
- If you are curling them, drape over a rolling pin while still warm and pliable.

CHEF'S TIP: If you make too much mixture, it will keep in the fridge for a week or can be frozen.

If you want to make coconut tuiles, substitute the plain flour for desiccated coconut.

143

petits fours

There are a number of ways to make chocolate curls; one of the most popular is to take elegant shavings from a block by using a vegetable peeler. Those are fine, as far as they go, but they are very small and a little unimaginative.

My favourite method of making them is to warm different types of good-quality chocolate: white, milk and dark. I pipe it through a very fine nozzle onto A4 acetate sheets (the type used to make overhead projector slides). The acetate sheets are transparent and can be washed and reused.

I'm not ashamed to use the microwave to melt my chocolate. Working in a busy restaurant means we have to save time – and the flavour and 'snap' of the chocolate are unaffected.

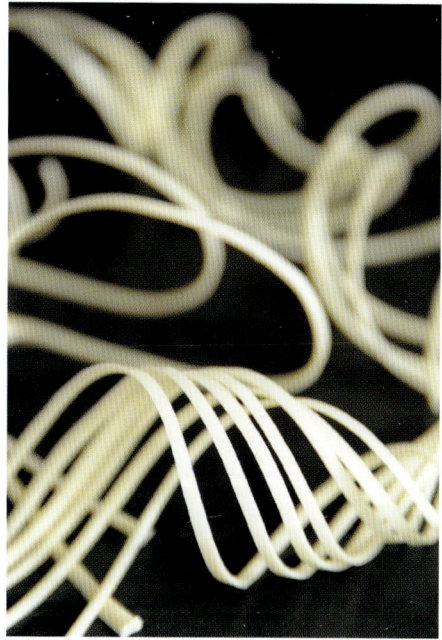

● Simply break your chocolate into small pieces and microwave in 15–20 seconds bursts, removing it from the machine and stirring until melted. The temperature should reach 54C for dark chocolate. Once it has melted, leave to cool and then reheat to 30C – it will still be liquid at that temperature and that is the time to pipe it.
● For milk chocolate, do exactly the same but heat to just 45C. Then cool, and reheat to 30C.
● For white chocolate, do the same but heat to just 38C. Then cool and reheat to 28C.
● Make a cone using greasproof paper, snip off the end and then pipe the chocolate onto the sheets, as shown in the photographs. Then fold the sheet back on itself from one end, to achieve your curl. You can make other shapes using a similar method.
● Leave to set in the fridge.

CHOCOLATE LOLLIPOPS

petits fours

These are a real treat. They are also very, very easy to make.

● Melt your chocolate as explained for chocolate curls (see page 145).
● Spoon the molten mixture onto a heatproof mat to create a small circle.
● Now add in a lollipop stick and garnish with whatever flavourings you like. Use pieces of dried fruit, such cranberry or mango, as well as plenty of chopped nuts, maybe pistachio and almond, or walnut and hazelnut.
● Leave to set in the fridge. It couldn't be simpler, and your guests will all be left wanting more!

MACAROONS

petits fours

I'm a huge fan of macaroons. But, like all pastry chefs, I know how tricky they are to make. There is no failsafe method. Different ovens, different quality ingredients and different atmospheric conditions all seem to influence the outcome – so be prepared to be patient. You're unlikely to get it right first time – and if you do, I may well offer you a job in my kitchen!

Experiment with different flavourings and colourings. And don't be afraid to add small dots of candy, or other garnishes, to the end result.

INGREDIENTS
125g ground almonds
225g icing sugar
4 egg whites
Pinch of cream of tartar
25g caster sugar

FOR A PLAIN CHOCOLATE BUTTER CREAM FILLING
2 tbsp milk
110g soft butter
170g icing sugar
55g cocoa powder

METHOD
● Put the icing sugar and ground almonds together into the blender and blitz into a fine powder, then sieve.

● Whisk the egg whites until soft peaks form. Work in the caster sugar and cream of tartar. Do not overwhip.

● If you want to add colour, add a colour gel to the egg white. Use natural food colouring – gels are essential. If you use liquid colouring, you will spoil the recipe.

● Fold the dry ingredients into the egg whites and form a smooth paste. Pipe the paste through a plain nozzle. You can choose the size and shape you want, though a 1.5cm nozzle is good. Leave to rest for at least two hours, so that a thin skin forms on the top of the paste. You can test whether or not they are ready by touching the side of the macaroon. If there is no give then they are ready.

● Pipe onto a lined baking tray and bake at 160C for 15 minutes, though the timing can vary. You should see the macaroon rise up, through the window of your oven. Once it's risen, turn the temperature down to 120C. Now cook for about an hour, until dried through. (The method is similar to making meringue. The exact cooking time will depend on the size of the macaroon. When you lift it up from your baking tray, it shouldn't stick to the tray.)

● For the filling, beat the ingredients together and then pipe onto the flat side of your macaroon shells and sandwich them together.

CHEF'S TIP: If you want a strawberry butter cream, substitute the cocoa powder for 1 tsp of strawberry purée. Use your imagination to flavour your butter cream. Use pistachio or a range of different fruit and nut fillings.

CHOCOLATE TRUFFLES

petits fours

I use a basic chocolate ganache recipe and then add all manner of colourful flavours and textures to my end-of-dinner truffles.

I've included six of my favourites here, though you can be as creative as you wish with yours. If you have a predilection for a particular fruit, then turn it to a dust by creating fruit crisps (follow the pineapple crisp recipe from page 119) and then blitz in a processor. The options are endless.

INGREDIENTS

500g dark chocolate – 70%-plus
60g soft brown sugar
10g honey
75g cubed butter
435ml double cream

METHOD

- Heat the chocolate over a bain-marie. While it's melting, boil the honey with the soft brown sugar and cream together. Once boiling remove from the heat.
- Add into the melted chocolate and mix, to make an emulsion, then stir in the butter until it has melted and leave to set for an hour. After an hour, it should be cool but you'll still be able to pipe it.
- Line a chopping board with baking parchment and pipe the truffles onto it.

TOPPINGS

Cocoa powder. Use a good quality powder (eg Valrhona) and dust lightly.

Meringue and macaroon crumb. Simply break up surplus meringues and macaroons into a dust and then dredge your truffles. It's a great way to add colour and texture.

Dessicated coconut. Add a natural food colour to it, or a food gel. Rub the coconut and gel together, until the colour is evenly distributed, then apply.

Ground pistachio nut. I love the vibrant colour, the warm nutty taste and the texture that ground pistachio nuts give.

Flaked chopped almonds. Make sure the pieces aren't too big, otherwise they will fall off.

Praline. Heat 100g of normal sugar with a tablespoon of water over a gentle heat until you have a caramel. It should be a light golden colour. Now add 50g of hazlenuts. Leave to set. When cool, break up and then blitz.

decoration

I'm a huge fan of carving: I love to make dragons, flowers and other ornamentations from watermelons, mango, beetroot, sweet pepper, carrot and other root vegetables. Adding a garnish seems to tell people that you have gone to a lot of time and trouble to make them feel welcome; it shows them that you've gone the extra mile.

I've spent a lifetime learning how to carve fruit and vegetables and it is a technique that you can improve upon over time. You need to observe a number of golden rules before you get started: make sure the watermelon is clean and your knives are clean and sharp too. Your fruit should be at room temperature: if it's come straight from the fridge it will be harder to work. If you intend to prepare your carving before your guests arrive, then pop the finished piece back into the fridge after cutting and before serving.

There are other good tips to observe: make sure you cut away the bottom of your watermelon, so that you can stabilise the fruit while you are working. Also, make sure you work on a flat surface.

As a beginner, it is probably best to draw the design onto the watermelon rind with a fine pencil, so you can see what you are doing as you go. Now gently cut through the rind and work away until you've completed your masterpiece. As you progress, you'll be able to do it without the use of a design.

SUGAR RIBBON (ABOVE) AND SUGAR BASKET

154 COOK THAI WITH SUREE COATES

CHOCOLATE BOW   **SUGAR HEART**

I love to experiment with sugar and chocolate; it helps me to create extra-special dishes. On St Valentine's Day, you can create red sugar hearts, by heating sugar and adding red food gel, then creating shapes on a heatproof mat.

Spun-sugar baskets are slightly more complicated, though they're not that difficult. Melt 500g of caster sugar in a pan and add 100ml of cold water and a tablespoon of glucose syrup. Heat the ingredients in a heavy-bottomed pan until you have a caramel (and resist the temptation to stir or shake, otherwise you'll get sugar crystals). Boil to approximately 180C and then use a fork to drizzle the molten sugar onto the back of a ladle. Alternatively, form thin strands over a steel sharpener, then form a delicate ball in your hands. If the caramel hardens, place over a warm heat. Be careful when you are cooking this: the caramel reaches 185C, which can cause serious burns.

Sugar ribbons are a real treat. They can be coloured and flavour in any way you like – but they do take a lot of practice. I could fill another book with lessons on sugarcraft: it's something that you never stop learning about. The process is simple, in essence. You make a sugar syrup and then transfer to a heatproof surface. After a minute or two, the sugar cools and becomes pliable: that's when you can work it. If the sugar hardens, you can pop it into the microwave for a short time to soften it again. Gently working the pliable sugar with your hands enables you to make incredible ribbons and shapes.

Chocolate bows are another favourite. They're made in a very similar way to chocolate curls, by adding together rows and rows of white and dark chocolate. The effect is simply stunning.

Index of recipes

Aubergine and chinese sausage fried rice 96
Banana fritter with coconut ice-cream 124
Beef with mushroom in oyster sauce 88
Beef with udon noodle and sesame seed. 98
Blueberry cheesecake with white chocolate sauce 132
Calamari 36
Chicken fried rice 104
Chicken satay with rice noodle cake 100
Chicken satay 42
Chicken with chilli and ginger 90
Chilli chocolate tart with coconut sorbet and chocolate-dipped chilli 134
Chocolate curls. 144
Chocolate lollipops. 146
Chocolate truffles. 150
Coconut panna cotta with exotic fruits 120
Crispy cod with sweet-and-sour sauce and cherry tomatoes 64
Cucumber vinaigrette 18
Duck with lychees and cherry tomatoes in a red curry sauce. 84
Duck with orange sauce. 82
Egg fried rice. 102
Exotic fruit tower 126
Fish cakes 48
Fruit fools 130
Green curry paste. 21
Honeycomb 141
King prawns with egg noodle, beetroot noodle and
    sweet-and-sour sauce. 108
Lamb cutlets in sweet chilli sauce. 86
Lemon chicken 46
Lemon posset with shortbread and fruit 136
Macaroons 148
Massaman curry paste. 22
Massaman curry with beef 80
Minced pork with chilli and basil 92
Monkfish and prawn green thai curry with vegetables and fragrant rice . . .68

Mussels 52
Noodle soup with minced pork balls 30
Pad thai 110
Panang curry paste 23
Pineapple tart tatin with coconut sorbet and pineapple crisps 118
Pork dumpling with a dipping sauce 44
Pork with crispy noodle nests 112
Prawn fried rice 106
Prawn toasts with cucumber vinaigrette 32
Prawn, red gurnard and noodle in a coconut-and-lemongrass sauce 66
Red curry paste 20
Salmon teriyaki with wild-herb salad and vegetable batons 62
Satay dip 16
Sea bass with potato galette and wild black coconut rice 60
Sea bream and asparagus 56
Shortbread with rose petals 140
Sour curry 25
Spicy beef salad 50
Spicy chicken soup 28
Spicy king prawn soup 26
Spring rolls 40
Stir-fry pork with green vegetables 94
Sushi with diced pepper and pickled ginger 114
Sweet chilli dip 17
Sweet-and-sour sauce 19
Tempura vegetable with cucumber vinaigrette 34
Thai fish three ways, with wasabi sauce 70
Thai green curry with chicken 76
Thai red curry with chicken, mango and asparagus 78
Thai sticky black rice pudding with mango rose 122
Tuiles 142
Vegetable samosa with mango salad 38
Wrapped sole with asparagus, mushrooms and coconut-and-
    lemongrass sauce 58
Yellow curry paste 24

sourcing

Sourcing ingredients is hugely important. If you cook with good quality meat, vegetables, fish and spices, your food will taste great. If you cook with inferior quality ingredients, the flavours will also be inferior. It's worth investing a little time in finding good suppliers and sticking with them. It will help you if you can find a specialist oriental supermarket or grocer to supply some of the herbs and spices. Take the time to find ones that are local to you – you'll find such outlets dotted around the UK.

You might also be able to procure supplies from the ever-increasing number of online outlets.

We tend to try different suppliers because we're keen to find the best quality for our customers. There are a few, however, which are exceptional and on which we rely day in and day out. In Broseley, we have a great local butcher, Simon Gibbons, who supplies our meat. Simon is a master butcher and lets us know what's coming in so that we can feature it on our menu. He can trace his meat back to a specific farm, field and animal, so we know we are getting only the best.

I also use Birmingham Wholesale Market, which is exceptional. It's a vast complex and supplies the freshest produce. My husband Simon makes regular trips, sometimes at 3am in the morning. That way we make sure we have the freshest fish, right in from the boat.

The rules for produce are simple. If it costs a little bit more to buy the best, then go for it. You'll taste the difference.

acknowledgements

My biggest thanks go to Simon and Ross, my husband and son, for supporting me throughout my career. Their constant encouragement and support is the best motivation I could ever have. I always know when I've come up with a great new dish – by the smiles on their faces.

I'm also very grateful to Simon's mother, Joan Shepherd, for her support for this project. She helped us to get started and has been incredibly loyal and generous in making sure it came to fruition.

I would like to thank James Day, from www.leisuremarketingltd.co.uk, who has been extremely supportive of my career in recent years. James has helped to bring my work to a bigger audience and has been instrumental in gaining me wider recognition.

Adam Haynes designed this book and helped us to realise our creative vision. I hope you'll agree, he's given the book a real 'wow factor'. His designs have been clean, sophisticated and uncluttered, and we're grateful.

Finally, I'd like to thank Andy Richardson, who managed the project and worked in a variety of roles. I'm sure he nicked the chicken satay following one photoshoot, but I'll forgive him!